Start & Run a Tattoo & Body Piercing Studio

Start & Run a Tattoo & Body Piercing Studio

Kurtis Mueller and Tanya Lee Howe

Self-Counsel Press
(a division of)
International Self-Counsel Press Ltd.
USA   Canada

Self-Counsel Press acknowledges the financial support of the Government of Canada through the Canada Book Fund (CBF) for our publishing activities.

Printed in Canada.

First edition: 2011

Library and Archives Canada Cataloguing in Publication

Mueller, Kurtis
    Start & run a tattoo and body piercing studio / Kurtis Mueller and Tanya Lee Howe.

Accompanied by CD-ROM.
ISBN 978-1-77040-070-2

    1. Tattooing. 2. Body piercing. 3. New business enterprises. I. Howe, Tanya Lee II. Title. III. Title: Start and run a tattoo and body piercing business.

GT2345.M83 2011   391.6'5   C2010-906869-6

Cover Image
Copyright©iStockphoto/Angel kisses/TAPshooter

Inside Images
Copyright©iStockphoto/Tattoo Grunge Elements/mxtama

Self-Counsel Press
(a division of)
International Self-Counsel Press Ltd.

1704 North State Street	1481 Charlotte Road
Bellingham, WA 98225	North Vancouver, BC V7J 1H1
USA	Canada

Contents

10 𝕳iring 𝔅ody 𝔓iercers

Samples

Worksheet

Notice to Readers

Laws are constantly changing. Every effort is made to keep this publication as current as possible. However, the authors, the publisher, and the vendor of this book make no representations or warranties regarding the outcome or the use to which the information in this book is put and are not assuming any liability for any claims, losses, or damages arising out of the use of this book. The reader should not rely on the authors or the publisher of this book for any professional advice. Please be sure that you have the most recent edition.

Note: The fees quoted in this book are correct at the date of publication. However, fees are subject to change without notice. For current fees, please check with the court registry or appropriate government office nearest you.

Prices, commissions, fees, and other costs mentioned in the text or shown in samples in this book may not reflect real costs where you live. Inflation and other factors, including geography, can cause the costs you might encounter to be much higher or even much lower than those we show. The dollar amounts shown are simply intended as representative examples.

Acknowledgments

Kurtis Mueller: First and foremost I'd like to offer my thanks to my wonderful wife, Heather Mueller. Her belief in me and my ideas has given me the strength and determination to be successful. Our idea to open an ethical and professional studio ten years ago led to this book and a very successful business.

Thanks to my Mom, Rosemary Mueller; Dad, Doug Mueller; and brother, Blaine Mueller, whose support has been amazing.

Thanks to my co-author and editor Tanya Howe, whose idea for this book made it possible.

Also, I would like to thank the staff of Jaded over the years for the ideas they have imparted and the lessons I have learned from them. A final thanks to the people of Self-Counsel Press

for their belief in this book; their support has been terrific!

Tanya Howe: I'd like to thank Jackie Anderson Lea and the many others who recommended Jaded Body Arts. If it wasn't for those recommendations, I would never have met Lori Thurlow and found out what a great owner Kurtis Mueller is. A big thanks to Lori for being a wonderful and friendly artist who provided me with the initial insight into the business and helped inspire me to talk to Kurtis about writing this book. (Also, for her fantastic work creating my tattoos!)

My goal was to understand this industry that keeps its secrets so close. Kurtis was a wonderful co-writer and he provided me with insight into the industry. I have had a love of tattoos since I was a teenager so co-writing this book with Kurtis was a dream come true!

A huge thank you goes to Eileen Velthuis (also known as Evil E) for being a fantastic managing editor and friend — without you, this book wouldn't have been possible. Thanks to Richard Day for taking a chance on me so many years ago as a young intern editor, and to Diana Douglas for having a publishing house that publishes wonderful informative guides. I would be remiss if I didn't mention Lisa Fuentes for doing the great cover design of this book.

Thanks to my father, Al Janzen, and mother, Pam Janzen, for being so supportive of me over the years and encouraging me to write this book. Thanks goes to my hubby for insisting I "start writing or find a new career"! A very special thank you goes to my Auntie Lorita for always being there for me.

Kurtis and Tanya: We would also both like to thank Lori Thurlow and Tatianna Adams for providing us with some great tattoo art to display on the CD; as well as Kristen Low and Micheal Bryce Ward for providing pictures of their piercings for the CD.

Introduction

"You want to open a tattoo studio?" This was the question most people asked me with some level of bewilderment almost a decade ago when I was opening my first shop. I had management skills, and although I had received training as a piercer, I had no skill set as a tattoo artist, which was certainly not the norm in the industry at the time. To those who questioned me, I replied, "Times are changing." I was determined to be the one to bring that change to the tattoo community.

Back when I opened my shop the industry resembled more of an elitist club than a business, as there were and still are minimal regulations in the United States and Canada. In the last ten years this has changed dramatically in regards to elitism. Now anyone from artists to entrepreneurs — even celebrities — are opening studios. I have seen many positive changes within the tattoo and piercing world during this period of time, such as some increased regulation of current sterilization procedures, upscale interiors, and a focus on customer service. Though body modification has been practiced throughout history by various cultures and civilizations, in the last decade it has become more widely accepted by mainstream North American society.

You can find tattoo motifs on virtually everything these days, from underclothes to home decor and even in toy stores, a move that is definably attributed to a shift in society's perception of the industry. I once read a quote that stated, "Tattoos aren't just for sailors, bikers, and prostitutes anymore." The variation in clientele — everyone from professionals to grandmothers — definitely attests to the uniqueness of the various forms of body modification. Popular shows such as *Inked*, *Miami Ink*, *LA Ink*, and *London Ink* have all helped bring tattooing into the mainstream population. Regardless of the popularity, I believe as with starting any business a true interest for the work must be present — a reason beyond making a profit, or boosting the ego.

For me, opening my business was about the art, the people, and the belief that I could bring more to the industry because I looked at it from a business perspective while maintaining a respect for the art and culture of tattooing. It was my dream that the artistic value of tattoos and piercings be showcased in a positive environment for the artists and the clients. Though it is an industry that can be portrayed to have a quazi-rockstar persona for the artists and owners of shops, the reality behind each successful tattoo shop is a lot of long hours, hard work, and self-motivation to continually produce quality artwork and attract clients.

Part of the responsibility that artists in my studio have is educating their clientele about safe body art. Leading by example, I have taken on that responsibility as an owner to educate my community by teaching safe body art to high school groups and youth facilities. This came about from the health officials deciding they were going to add a safe body art component to a program they were running in high schools about risks.

The health board secretly sent around representatives to every tattoo and piercing studio in the city. They posed as clients and asked for a tour of our facility along with loads of questions. The next day the "customer" I had helped came back and told me that she was an administrator for the health board and they were inconspicuously "interviewing" all of the tattoo and piercing studios to see which one would be the best representative to teach safe body art. I was honored by the offer of being the chosen representative. It was because of our knowledge and commitment to providing the best experience possible that we were selected. Needless to say, for a fledgling business the opportunity provided a more positive image and reputation than any amount of advertising could have given us. It also verified that my concepts for creating a higher level of professionalism within the industry locally had paid off. This is, in part, why I believe there is always something new to learn within the industry, and researching new methods and executing them for the betterment of both my clients' experience and my artists' abilities has always been a priority for me as an owner. Because of this priority, I have included health-related information in this book to help keep our industry clean and safe.

With the tattoo industry gaining such notoriety you will be hard pressed to find a town or city that does not have at least one studio already operating, so you will have to make sure what you plan to offer is different and innovative. It is helpful to find your own niche, something not already offered by other studios in your area, and focus on it. Competition between studios can be fierce or friendly, depending on the location, so be prepared to have a thick skin. You will also find that keeping on top of the industry and new developments is an asset to this type of business, which will also be discussed in this book.

To enter into the tattoo and piercing industry, it is a necessity to be artistically talented or creative. It is not enough to think it would be a cool job because you have a few tattoos or piercings. To view a studio as only a business or, worse yet, as a status symbol, would be to operate at only half of its potential. I have seen a few shops open and close within six months because they employed that kind of mentality. A tattoo studio can be a very rewarding venture, but is certainly not for the faint of heart.

This industry has little to no franchises as of yet so there is still room for small businesses to operate. This fact allows more uniqueness between studios within the tattoo and piercing world.

Coming from a background in economic development, I knew my ideas could be highly profitable if I was willing to put in the effort to maintain a higher standard. There are many benefits to opening a tattoo and piercing studio and my experience in doing so has taught me many valuable lessons. The journey has not been without its own sets of trials and tribulations which at times have been very stressful. Some of the unexpected trials have entailed theft by employees, the stress of worrying if the staff is making enough money, and if they are happy with their jobs. There is a constant burden of wondering how the business is doing even when I am on a vacation or just at home for the evening, not to mention the balancing act of trying to keep artists adhering to a schedule and rules while allowing their creative talents to flow. However, the fulfillment I feel, knowing I have created a successful business, is a feeling that is hard to match.

By owning your own tattoo studio you will get to see your ideas and concepts come to life through hard work and determination, which is very rewarding. To be the one making all the decisions can be the most empowering or the most deflating experience.

The best parts of this industry are the people I have met, the artistic ideas that have transpired between the clients and the artists, and watching everything come to fruition. This industry's acceptance and embracing of new ideas of body modification never ceases to amaze me. Being witness to the tears of joy when a memorial tattoo is finished or to see a group of people come out of the piercing room full of laughter and excitement is a true perk of the job.

There are also the comical moments. One of the most off-the-wall concepts that I have had the privilege to bear witness to was a urinal back piece, like the ones you find in a public men's washroom, covering the entire back, complete with the urinal cake!

I would recommend that anyone thinking of opening a tattoo and piercing studio really understand the process of tattooing and piercing. It can be very involved and more demanding than one might think, and to not understand it could result in many problems.

Throughout this book we will discuss the various steps to opening, running, and maintaining a successful tattoo and piercing studio, while highlighting the important aspects particular to this industry. In writing this book, our hope is that you, the reader, will open a studio that benefits the tattoo and piercing industry. Opening a clean, organized, and safe studio will benefit the industry as a whole and it will also benefit your business.

You will find many books out there on how to become a tattoo apprentice and they will go into detail about the industry from that perspective. This book is from the perspective of a successful business owner and it will help you start your own studio from the beginning. This book will help you get on the right track to running a successful tattoo and body piercing studio.

The CD included with this book contains some work from the artists that have worked at Jaded Body Arts Inc., along with links to information to further your understanding of the tattoo industry and the regulations and health codes for many areas across the United States and Canada. We hope to encourage strong morals and ethics in regards to the procedures used to perform the tattoos and piercings in your studio. The CD also includes worksheets to help keep your business organized.

Is This Business Right for You?

In most areas in North America, you don't need to be an artist or piercer to start and run your own tattoo and body piercing business. However, you do need to do the research and have an understanding and respect for the industry in order to make it.

Many studios fail due to the owner's lack of business skills. Many artistic types of people are not cut out to do the business side, just like not all businesspeople are qualified to become tattoo artists or body piercers. Starting and running a business requires just as much skill as the services (i.e., tattooing and piercing) you are offering to clients. A balanced combination of understanding business aspects as well as

the artistry is crucial in this industry. If you are getting into this industry just for the money or lifestyle, then your business may be doomed from the beginning. You need to love what goes into creating the art and understand how to run a business in order to succeed.

The tattooing and piercing industry can be very competitive and territorial. Note that if you are opening the studio as a businessperson as opposed to a businessperson/artist, you may not get a lot of support, understanding, or information from others in the industry. Also note that in some locations in North America, you cannot own a studio without having at least a 50 percent partnership with someone who is a licensed tattoo artist. You can find this information by reading the regulations set out by your state or provincial government. The website EveryTattoo.com includes information about each state's laws; however, for the most up-to-date information, check with your state or provincial government.

Your decisions and responsibilities in this industry reach far beyond what type of advertising to choose or what decor to go with; the reality is your decisions could result in infections to clients, allergic reactions, severe illness, or in some extreme instances, death. Tattooing and piercing should be viewed as minor surgical procedures by the artists, piercers, support staff, and owner.

Also, many moral and ethical decisions will be encountered, such as whether to allow faces to be tattooed, whether to allow names to be tattooed, whether you will purchase a lower-quality ink that contains heavy metals even though it is legal but will limit the customer from ever having a medical MRI in the future. What about purchasing body jewelry that contains nickel because it's less expensive, even though most people have an allergy to nickel? These are just a few of the many decisions you will need to consider when opening your studio.

Passion may keep you interested but you should continually be looking for ways to improve and grow your business. This in turn leads to success and innovation. When people think that they know everything is most often when failure occurs.

Before you begin writing your business plan (as discussed in Chapter 3), consider the topics in this chapter. You need to know if this is the right business for you. Motivation, thick skin, connections in the industry, financial savings, and support from others are all things you will need to get started and to continue if you want to succeed.

1. You Must Have Motivation

It can take two years or more before you finally make a profit. So you will need to have the motivation to stick with it until you can make money for all your hard work.

When you are setting up your business you will put in a lot of long hours. When you finally open the doors the long hours will continue until you can afford to hire the staff to help you. Many new business owners suffer burnout from the effort and stress involved in setting up and then running a business. Be prepared mentally for this strain.

Take a good hard look at what type of worker you are. Are you self-motivated or do you need someone to push you to get things done? If you are not self-motivated, and you have a lot of tasks left undone in your current job or home life, this may be an indicator that you will not perform well as a business owner.

If you don't understand how to do something, will you do research to find out how to go about the task the right way or will you just wing it and hope for the best? If you are serious about opening a business, then you will need to do the research. Reading this book is a good start, but you will still have to find out information after reading it, such as what are the health regulations in your area? What are the zoning laws? What type of insurance do you need? These are all questions you need to find answers for among many more, in order to open your business and make it a success.

In your current job, do you need praise in order to feel motivated? As a business owner, you will not have a boss to give you praise. Instead, you will need to make sure your business is running smoothly and that your clients return happy in order for you to feel like you are doing a good job. Some days will be hard and filled with complaining customers, while other days you may find your customers filled with the joy of having a beautiful piece of art on their skin.

2. You Must Have Thick Skin

Not everyone will be happy that you are opening up shop in their neighborhood. You may have opposition. It is not unusual for people to protest something they don't understand or support. How will you deal with protestors outside your shop demanding you shut down your business?

What if you found the perfect location to rent in a strip mall, but the neighboring businesses refuse to allow the landlord to rent to you? Will you get mad and yell at them or will you try to talk to them about it? Maybe you will have to consider a different location and let that place go. (See Chapter 2 for more information on finding a good location.)

You may also encounter criticism from others in the industry who do not want a similar business setting up shop in the same area or city. How will you make your studio different or get along with others in the same industry located in the same area?

As mainstream as the industry has become in recent years, there is still a fair amount of stigma attached to operating or working at a studio. How will you deal with the prejudices and opinions of other people when you tell them what type of business you own? As an owner you are the frontperson of your business. Always. No matter where you are, your responses and interactions will have direct impact on your business.

As you can see, you need a thick skin to start up and successfully run a tattoo and body piercing studio. This type of business, more than other small businesses, can have a lot of unexpected challenges. However, if you are determined and have a plan, then you can get through any opposition you face.

3. The Importance of Connections in the Industry

Connections in the tattoo and body piercing world are important. You need to find good artists. Businesspeople who lack artistic talent themselves may have a harder time attracting artists to work in their studios as they may lack an understanding of the needs and requirements of the artists. However, many artists like to concentrate on the artwork and not the business aspects, so you may find some artists that are willing to work for you doing the creative work while you deal with the paperwork.

A new studio may have trouble attracting veteran artists due to the fact that it's new and hasn't proven itself yet. It may be easier to hire newer artists who need a break into the industry, but you will still need to know where to find good artists. So where do you begin?

You begin by researching the industry and finding connections and places that advertise for artists looking for work. You also have to consider whether the artists will bring a client base. If they are extremely new to the industry themselves, then you can't count on them having an already established clientele. (See Chapters 9 and 10 for more information about finding artists and piercers.)

Networking, getting to know people in the industry, going to tattoo conventions, and talking to other owners may provide you with some valuable connections. Having a general interest in learning and wanting to improve the industry where you're living will also go a long way to ensuring you receive proper information from associates. Know where your information is coming from and back it up with your own research. A caveat: It is not unheard of for existing shops to attempt to sabotage new shops at start-up.

4. Be Prepared Financially

The most negative aspect to opening your own studio is the risk. For example, the risk of losing all your hard-earned investment (i.e., bankruptcy), and having wasted hours of time and effort only to be left with nothing and still owing money. For some individuals this can cause serious mental and physical setbacks, and deepening of the financial loss over time.

Another negative aspect is the unpredictability of income; basically how money will come in and when. When you cannot determine your cash flow, making a budget or just paying the bills can be difficult and extremely stressful.

Determining start-up costs is a difficult task; it is a good idea to have at least three to six months of money to carry you if minimal money comes in. Also note the unpaid hours you spend to start up a business will reach into the hundreds.

Unless you are independently wealthy you will probably have to make some lifestyle adjustments, meaning cutbacks to your personal spending from the start, until clients are gained and revenue starts coming in. Statistics have proven time and time again that the failure rate of new businesses is much higher than for existing ones. Lack of staff at the beginning can be difficult if you become ill or need time off, because there will be no one to cover for you if you cannot afford to close the business for that time.

It is almost impossible to dedicate the time needed to open a new studio if you have a current full-time job. But if your new business is not making money, how do you pay the bills at the business and at home?

One of the last hurdles to consider is the amount of effort and sheer number of things that need to be completed in a timely manner to open; it is intense to say the least. Costs will quickly add up and so will the pressure to do everything right.

See Chapters 3 and 4 for more information on business planning and financials.

5. Have a Support System

In starting a new business you must have the support of your partner or spouse if you have one, as this endeavor will also change his or her life. The extremely long hours spent in the first few years are intense, as are the many stressful situations that will be encountered, not to mention the financial stress at the start. Without your partner truly supporting you, failure of your business or relationship could be possible.

Having someone listen to you vent about the business, or give you advice and help you solve problems may be what you need to keep you motivated and moving forward in your plans. Also, having someone there to celebrate and remind you of the small and big rewards of a job well done can be a great way to keep you going when times are tough.

2
Finding a Good Location

Finding a good location may be one of the biggest challenges you will face when opening your studio. Even though tattoos and piercings have become more accepted by society there are still places that will not be rented to you because landlords or neighbors perceive this type of industry negatively. The city you want to set up shop in may also have strict zoning regulations that will prevent you from opening your business in the most ideal location for your chosen clientele.

When Kurtis opened his studio almost a decade ago, he was turned down by eight potential locations because of the type of business he wanted to open. For example, he had found the perfect storefront (also known as a bay), with a good location for the clients he wanted to target. The landlord was willing to rent it to him, but the landlord's tenants beside the bay had been there for years and said they would move their businesses if a tattoo and piercing studio moved in beside them. In another instance Kurtis found a good bay, and while the existing neighboring businesses had no problem with a tattoo studio, the landlord did.

The city Kurtis' studio is currently in has three shopping malls; the biggest, newest, and most popular of the three will never let a tattoo and piercing studio rent a bay in their mall as the owners feel it will drive away families and attract an unwelcome element. If you think you've found the perfect location, keep in mind that you might not be accepted or even considered.

1. Research the Market

The first step to finding a good location is to research the market. Obtain population statistics from the city you are considering — all the research has been done by the government so all you have to do is access it. It is a general rule of thumb that you should have at least 20,000 residents per studio, so in a city of 100,000 five studios would be okay, but any more studios would mean less money is made by the existing studios, or somebody will go out of business. This, of course, is a general number and can fluctuate, but the fluctuation happens mostly in tourist towns where it is not unusual to find two or three studios per 20,000 residents. Another situation in which more studios can exist is in university and college towns where huge population jumps occur; also note this segment of the population is a main demographic for tattoo and piercing studios.

If you are planning on opening in an area that has more than one studio per 20,000 residents, you will want to make sure that your studio is going to offer something different than the others. Can you fill a niche market? If you are already a tattooist or a piercer, do you have enough clients willing to follow you to your new studio? If you feel that you do have enough clients, take the total number of clients you tattoo or pierce and subtract approximately 25 percent from this number because this percentage of clients will stay with the current studio as opposed to following the artist to a new location.

Visit all the studios in the area, or as many as you can before opening. This will give you great insight into what is offered by the other studios. Deciding what type of studio to open in terms of design and the clients desired may depend on what is offered or not offered by other studios. The popularity of tattoo and piercing studios has been steadily climbing for the last 20 years with women being the highest contributors to this number. About six years ago the tattoo and piercing industry was in the top ten fastest growing industries and it is still continuing to expand and grow.

Research the city in which you wish to be located and its demographics. If there is a high population of seniors, you might want to make sure that you will have enough business from your target market as seniors do not generally frequent tattoo and piercing studios. Also, if you are locating in a tourist town, consider what type of tourism exists. For example, is it seasonal? If so, will you be able to make enough money to make it through the "dead" season? Almost all landlords, even in tourist locations, will not rent for only the summer or busy months; the lease on the building will be applied for a year or more.

State and provincial governments offer excellent statistics on spending patterns of the residents in certain areas as well as demographics and population trends, which is very useful information when you are considering a location for your studio. Since tattooing and piercing are not necessities and are considered luxury items, researching the disposable income in the area is very beneficial. Get as many statistics as you can because this will remove some of the guesswork for forecasting revenue and expenses.

2. Things to Consider When Choosing a Location

Location will set the image and feel of the studio. Tattoo and piercing studios are one of the most varied of any types of business in terms of location. You will find them everywhere from high-class shopping districts, to downtowns, to box-store outlet locations, malls, "seedy" areas, skateboard shops, casinos, tropical destinations, and everything in between. Tattoo studios are not completely location-driven, meaning that clients will travel to the studio even if it is not close or convenient. A good studio will attract business wherever it might be.

2.1 Proximity to the competition

The proximity of tattoo and piercing studios varies from city to city. Usually you will find that the majority of tattoo studios try to spread themselves out from each other, covering a variety of areas throughout the city to reach different clients. This rule is broken in tourist towns where the studios will be clustered together in trendy shopping districts or on popular streets where there could be upward of four studios within a three-block radius.

Having a healthy distance between you and your competition is generally beneficial as this will somewhat prevent price checking, which is when clients go to a few studios with the same drawing and then pick the least expensive studio. This practice by clients is made more difficult when the studios are spread apart and driving is required. (See Chapter 7 for more information on pricing your services.)

2.2 Consider your clientele

The most beneficial location for your studio depends on what type of clients you are targeting. If you want to attract families, pick a safe location that families frequent such as big-box store areas, neighborhood strip malls with a grocery store, or other businesses frequented by families. If you want to attract younger clients in the 18 to 25 age range, pick a location such as a shopping mall or trendy shopping district. You may want a more adult clientele, so good areas to look at would be a nightclub district or a strip mall with more adult-centered stores.

To a degree, location will also determine the hours your business is open to the public. In a daytime shopping area you might want to keep with business hours in the area and open early and close early. In a nightclub district you will want to open later and close later.

2.3 Availability of parking and transportation

When you consider a location, always check to see what type of parking is available for your clients. Tattoo appointments can be upward of two hours, so parking is very important. If parking is scarce, your clients may not be happy to have to walk long distances to get to your studio, which means potential clients might just keep driving instead. If you can validate parking for your clients, do so because parking is a major issue for everyone that drives.

Another thing to consider is whether your business will be close to transportation such as bus stops or areas with a high volume of taxis. In bigger cities, the trend is going toward a green environment with less people driving personal vehicles. You want to make sure your business is always easy to get to no matter how your clients arrive.

2.4 Zoning regulations

Depending on your location, there might be restrictions in place that allow certain businesses to operate while others are not allowed. For zoning laws in your area, contact your city's zoning and planning department to find out if any restrictions apply. This can be extremely useful in saving time because you will not need to look at rental bays that you are not allowed to lease due to zoning laws.

Note that some city zoning regulations in the United States do not allow tattoo shops to exist within the city limits, so make sure you talk to your city officials before you rent or buy property for your business.

If you are opening a home-based studio, check the city's bylaws to make sure the city allows businesses in your residential area; parking will be one of the main determining factors. In most municipalities, to open a home-based business that will have clients coming and going, a certain majority of the residents in that area must approve the business. In our municipality, the approval rate is 70 percent or higher. It is a daunting and near impossible task to achieve this majority in most neighborhoods because of the somewhat remaining perception that the tattoo and piercing industry is undesirable.

2.5 Health and safety regulations

When choosing a location, make sure you find out what the health-board regulations in your area require. Things you may need to consider are the room size, sink placements, ventilation, sterilization room requirements, and flooring. Any alterations to the site will depend on whether you are renting and are able to upgrade the facility in order to meet health codes. Also, consider the costs to do the alterations. When you are just starting a business, major renovations could set you back financially. (See Chapter 6 for more information on health regulations.)

You will never find a restaurant with a tattoo studio located in it. Tattooing and piercing cannot take place on the same premises in which food and beverages are served. To be approved to open a tattoo studio in a nightclub is extremely difficult even if you can find a health board that will permit this. The studio will have to have a separate entrance other than the nightclub entrance and it will have to be enclosed. Absolutely no alcoholic beverages will be allowed in the studio.

3. Negotiating a Commercial Lease

Many people underestimate the complexity of negotiating a commercial lease. If you plan to negotiate the lease yourself, be sure to do your research using the Internet, the library, and bookstores. Also talk to other people that are familiar with negotiating a commercial lease because they may be able to help you by giving you tips on how to negotiate properly, which will result in a better lease contract for you and your business. Self-Counsel Press also publishes a do-it-yourself kit titled *Commercial Lease Agreement*.

The lease is one of the most important legal documents you will sign, and it will have the most impact if you ever have to close your business. Even if you create the contract yourself, you will need a lawyer to sign the lease agreement before it is valid. It is recommended that you do get legal advice when making the contract. Another method is to hire a commercial real estate agent. This is a good approach to use as it is at no cost to the lessee.

A commercial lease agreement will consist of price per square foot, length of lease in months or years, property tax per year or month that is generally not included in the price per square foot, and will make clear who is responsible for all repairs to the building. Most leases will also require you to carry general business liability insurance. (For more information about insurance see Chapter 5.) All of these factors will vary from city to city and landlord to landlord.

Note that if you lease in a shopping mall, its commercial lease agreement will also include a clause that states something along the lines such as if you are not open at the same time as the mall opens, you will be fined a monetary sum. There are also many other rules the mall may have in place for businesses.

In considering price per square foot, get an average of other comparable storefronts in the area and go from there. It is similar to buying or renting a house so shop around to compare costs and space.

In considering the length of the lease, look at property values as they usually go up, which means that the lease will also go up accordingly. Signing a five- or ten-year lease may seem overwhelming but just remind yourself that if you locked in at X amount of dollars per square foot for ten years, that is the rate you pay even if property values skyrocket. The only downside to this is if you go out of business and you are locked in to a ten-year lease, you will owe for all the remaining months on the lease. Some landlords offer a sublet option to a third party to pay the remainder, but some don't. You may want to negotiate a sublet option just to protect yourself if things don't work out. Also consider whether you want to expand your business in the future. You may eventually need more room, which might be a problem in the current location you are considering.

Locking in for a long-term lease also offers security as you will know that the renovations and advertising dollars spent on this location will not be in vain. When you sign a commercial lease agreement most landlords will offer something called leasehold improvements, which means the landlord will grant you X amount of dollars to improve the space in lieu of paying rent. The standard is three months of rent for this type of agreement. This can be a huge advantage when starting your business and money is tight.

Take this step of the process seriously and have the contract reviewed by a registered lawyer before signing; most agreements are more than 20 pages of legal jargon so they can be hard to understand.

4. Pros and Cons of Buying an Established Tattoo and Piercing Studio

In this industry, especially in today's age, you may find yourself presented with the option of buying an established tattoo and piercing studio. With so many studios opening, closing, and going up for sale, you may have the choice to buy or start a new one. In considering an established studio, the most important question to ask is: What is the reputation for this studio in the community?

When a tattoo and piercing studio develops a bad reputation, it is almost impossible to erase this image from the public's mind, no matter what amount is spent on advertising. New ownership or just doing an excellent or innovative job will not be enough to rid the public of this perception or erase the damage of the previous owner.

If the studio you are considering passes the reputation question and has a good or excellent reputation within the community, you will need to consider the questions in Worksheet 1. (The CD includes a printable worksheet so that you can write down your answers as you are gathering the information you need to make a decision.)

Take the price of the studio and compare this to what your start-up costs might be along with the time and stress involved in starting your business. Among the other points listed in Worksheet 1 on which the price of the studio will be based is something called "good will." Good will is the price that has been calculated for things such as effort and time invested, risks that were taken, and the money that had been invested to gain clients. This can be calculated by professionals that specialize in this and an accurate picture can be gained into

Worksheet 1
Questions to Ask before Buying an Established Studio

Questions to Ask before Buying an Established Studio

1. How long has it been in business?

2. What is the reputation of the studio in this community?

3. What equipment, medical supplies, and furniture will come with the studio? (Listing the items is a good idea because it will help you figure out what additional items you will need to purchase.)

4. Will the artists (independent contractors) be staying on when you take control?

5. Do the financial statements seem to be in order? (It is advised to spend the money and have a certified accountant review these documents.)

6. Does the business have a client list with contact information? If so, how many clients?

7. Does it come with a vendor list? Is the business on good terms with the vendors?

8. Is it in a good location? (Carefully consider the location because it will set the image of your studio to the public.)

9. Is the parking adequate?

10. Does the business have health-board approval or does it require any major improvements or changes?

11. Why is the current owner selling the studio?

SELF-COUNSEL PRESS — START & RUN A TATTOO & BODY PIERCING STUDIO/11

whether the price reflects the profits generated and the current customer base.

The following list includes some of the pros of buying an established tattoo and piercing studio:

* An existing client base means immediate revenue.

* No major health-code compliances should need to be met through improvements or renovations, which translates into lower start-up costs.

* The business might exist in a good location.

* Money, time, and energy can be directed into operations of the business rather than one time start-up costs such as major advertising campaigns, major renovations, or the purchasing of equipment.

* Less competition as you are buying an established operational business rather than opening in the same area and being in direct competition with other studios.

* A tattoo and piercing studio with a good or an excellent reputation can basically eliminate your advertising expenses.

* A list of vendors, if provided, can be useful because many companies offer discounts for years of ordering or for spending a certain amount of money. These discounts can go up to 25 percent so this should not be overlooked.

* If a business has existed more than five years, there are statistics that prove the chance of failure is significantly reduced as compared to a business that is at less than the five-year mark.

❀ Economic downturns affect an established business less than a new one.

The following list includes some of the cons of buying an established business:

❀ The previous studio may have had bad relations with vendors such as unpaid bills, so you could risk being billed for the previous owner's debt or the vendors might not sell to your business.

❀ The clients of tattoos and piercings require extensive aftercare and check-ups. Will the clients of the previous studio owner expect you to pay for and take time out of your day to check and maintain their body modifications at no charge? More than likely they will, since they have already paid the previous studio owner.

❀ Will the clients continue to frequent your establishment or will they follow the previous artist or owner? In the tattoo and piercing industry many clients will select the studio for a particular artist.

❀ If the studio has ever had a poor health-inspection report, has the public forgotten about it or will they carry that perception to your studio?

❀ There could be pending or future lawsuits as a result of the previous owner's actions. As well you could be legally responsible for outstanding bills, unused gift certificates, etc. If you do not pay the bills, you could develop bad credit and relations with your vendors. If you do not honor the gift certificates, you could lose clients.

❀ If you are keeping existing artists (staff), they may not agree with your methods and quit, which could make life difficult for you and you could lose clients.

❀ Is the current location beginning a negative economic transition or is an undesired element being planned for the area in the future, such as a major freeway, which will make access to your business difficult? For situations like this, check with City Hall to see future plans for the area.

The final downside to buying an established studio is the personal loss in satisfaction from not starting the business from the beginning and the lingering question, "Is the studio successful or not successful because of my leadership, or is it because of the previous owner?"

The greatest pro to starting your own studio as opposed to buying an established business is the complete control and satisfaction of creating something new and watching it grow and change. It is your own, something you created, your vision, your dream. There is no preconceived notion either positive or negative by the public, and you create the type of image you want. The sense of achievement is much greater when success is reached than when you buy an established studio. There are no clients that have prepaid work you must honor, no unpaid vendors, and no disgruntled clients.

The cost difference between starting your own business and buying an established one will not be that different. The average costs for starting your own studio would be in the range of $20,000 to $70,000 depending on the area and type of studio. Buying an established studio could cost anywhere from $20,000 up to $120,000 for a high-end studio in a great location with an established clientele and at least five years in operation. These figures do not reflect the purchase of land or a building, only leasing options.

3 Develop a Business Plan

The business plan is a comprehensive document that is created to describe the future of the business. Developing a business plan can be a long, tedious process but should not be overlooked or rushed. It can take weeks or months to create a business plan so make sure you take the time to create a good one. It is the tool that can plot your journey on the road to success or failure. Through this process you will learn more about your business, develop new and innovative ideas, as well as identify the weaknesses and strengths you have.

The business plan will allow you to plan for the future of your studio and identify potential problems that can and will arise. It is used to attract investors, suppliers, new hires, banks, and other lenders such as the government for the purposes of obtaining financing.

1. Reasons to Create a Business Plan

You should understand your business plan inside and out and be able to clearly understand why the business will succeed and how it is going to achieve success. If you require outside funding, the investor should understand right from the start what the business is and what the return will be. To do this you must support any claims and projections that you have made about the business — as well as knowing every detail concerning the business. Unrealistic financial projections will more than likely lose an investor's interest.

A typical business plan may consist of 20 pages, although some business plans can be 100 pages or more, depending on the purpose of the plan and the nature of the business. For a tattoo and body piercing studio about 15 to 25 pages will be more than enough.

There are so many business plan templates to choose from that it's confusing and daunting, so I would recommend finding government agencies that supply templates online. These agencies want your business to be successful because it makes their statistics look good, and your business will pay taxes so that benefits the government as well. In the United States and Canada, you can find excellent business plan templates, advice, and resources for no charge on government websites. (See the Resources section on the CD for links to some valuable sites.) The Internet has a lot of information on writing business plans and many templates as well.

You might consider hiring a consultant to write your business plan. However, it's best for you to write the plan and, once you have written it, ask a business advisor or accountant to review and refine it. Writing your own plan will help you know your business inside and out. Often entrepreneurs neither take the time, nor do they feel a business plan is necessary for their businesses to succeed. This could not be further from the truth, especially when starting the business.

A business plan allows you to prevent future problems and to identify growth opportunities. It is a tool used in the search for funding when you are starting your business. A business plan should be used to guide the business rather than be a strict manual to be adhered to and never wavered from. You will want to revisit your business plan every six months in the first two years and then on a yearly basis after that to make sure you are following it, or to make adjustments. Do not be scared to make revisions if they will benefit your business.

Entrepreneurial training is becoming a significant component of many learning institutions in response to the escalating numbers of business start-ups in North America. You may be able to find a government agency that teaches a free self-employment course. Some of these types of courses run for six weeks or more and can be most helpful for new business owners.

How to write a business plan is being taught to entrepreneurs more than ever before. It is critical that you know what you are doing before you do it since more than 70 percent of new businesses fail after the second year. As an owner of the business, knowing what to do with it is key to being in the 30 percent of businesses that do succeed after two years, and creating a well-executed business plan will enhance the odds that your studio will be one of those that succeed.

2. What Goes into a Business Plan

The following sections discuss what should go into your business plan. Some of these sections in your plan may be longer or shorter depending on the vision you have for your studio.

2.1 Executive summary

The executive summary is the introduction to a formal business plan. It summarizes the business proposition, key financial projections, where the business stands at present, and the elements that are critical for success. While you may be tempted to rush through this part, remember this is the first thing a potential investor will read. If your executive summary doesn't grab his or her attention, then he or she probably won't bother reading the rest of your plan.

Be brief; a good executive summary ranges from half a page to two pages; anything longer and you risk losing your reader's attention or appearing unfocused. A safe bet is to keep it around one page or less.

Although the executive summary leads off the business plan, it should be written last. That way, you can cull information from the rest of the report, and make certain there are no inconsistencies.

2.2 Mission and vision statements

A mission statement is one or two sentences describing a company's function, markets, and competitive advantages; a short written statement of your business goals and philosophies.

The mission statement should define who your primary customers are, identify the service and possible product you produce, and describe the area in which you will operate. Try creating a mission statement by writing in one sentence the purpose of your business. Remember, this is not a slogan so it does not have to be catchy, just accurate and precise.

The mission statement will show your employees and clients what your business is all about. If you are unclear about what you plan to offer, then your employees and clients will also be unclear. Helpful information to include is pricing, quality, growth potential, marketplace position, and how you plan to achieve your studio's goals.

Here is an example of a mission statement for a tattoo and piercing studio:

Our studio's aim is to provide quality tattoos and piercings in a comfortable, clean, and professional environment. We will accomplish this by hiring only qualified staff, and buying only quality ink, equipment, and jewelry, as well as choosing a location that targets young professionals.

Creating a vision statement is a way to articulate your dreams and hopes for your business. Unlike a mission statement, a vision statement is for you and the other members of your company, not for your customers or clients. It defines your dreams of success for your business in the future.

The following is an example of a vision statement for a tattoo and piercing studio:

My tattoo and piercing studio will be a benchmark of professionalism for all other studios in the industry and it will attract the best artists and piercers in the industry, along with media recognition.

2.3 History and background

The history and background section is the section in which you will want to give the investors or bank a good idea of who you are and why you will succeed in this endeavor. Information to include in this section entails:

- The origin of the idea for the business.
- Your education level and history.
- Other businesses you have worked for that are relevant to the business.
- Your area of expertise in the industry.
- Any relevant associations, clubs, or societies to which you belong.
- Your areas of weakness and how you plan to offset them.
- Your technical skills.

This section can be from a half to a full page or slightly longer depending on your experience.

2.4 Description of your business

The description of your business is where you offer more detail about the type of business you want to open, who your customers will be, and what the competitive advantage is.

The business description usually begins with a short description of the industry. When describing the industry, discuss the present outlook as well as future possibilities. You should also provide information on all the various markets within the industry, including any new products or developments that will benefit or adversely affect your business. Base all of your observations on reliable data and be sure to footnote sources of information. This is important if you're seeking funding because the investor or bank will want to know just how dependable your information is, and they will not risk money on assumptions or guesses.

2.5 Company values

In essence, your company values are what make customers choose your business instead of the competition. Customers will compare the values of your studio against those of your competitors when deciding where to take their business.

Try to make this section short and precise. Your company's values explain why customers should buy from you. If you can't sum up your values, chances are you won't be able to execute them.

You should target the clients you want with precise and unique solutions. This is about your customer, not you, so know your customer. Your company values should discuss only what is applicable to your clients and the value you can bring to them.

Values come in numerous forms such as money, time, convenience, quality, and aftercare products and services. By this stage you should have a firm grasp on what product or service you intend to offer, as well as who you believe will be your primary customer. It is advisable that you also identify the type of person who will be your secondary customer.

2.6 Operations and employees

A tattoo and piercing studio relies on an operational plan to show which person is in charge of what activities within the business. You need to show the ownership of the business in terms of the partners' individual shares and contributions to the business as well as identify the channels of direction from management. In other words, you will need to list the *decision makers* and *action takers* and their place in the business structure. The operations and employees section will also outline the number of employees you intend to hire, how you will manage them, and your estimated personnel costs.

Begin this section by outlining your own managerial experience and skills as well as those of your team members (if you already have a team formed), the roles each member will play, and any particular areas of strength or deficiency in your lineup. It's fine if you don't yet have a complete team in place when you write your plan. Simply use this section of your business plan to outline the organizational structure, complete with job descriptions, how you plan to recruit key team members, and what their respective responsibilities will be.

Summarize important employee regulations and policies. Details and examples of such policies may be included in the appendixes of your plan. If a certain quality is demanded by your studio regarding quality of ink, needles, medical supplies, and body jewelry, describe which suppliers you will allow and which ones you will not.

Remember to consider opportunity costs when placing an order. If you're selling a certain piece of body jewelry for $50 and you run out, every person who wanted that piece of jewelry and couldn't get one represents a missed opportunity of $50 in revenue. On the other side, if you order too many of the same piece of body jewelry, you'll be left with surplus inventory that might never sell. An accurate projection of the demand for your product is key to a successful operational strategy. The more focused your business concept is, the greater the likelihood that you'll attract investors and customers.

You will have to decide whether to hire your artists or piercers as subcontracted employees or put them on the payroll. There are many pros and cons to subcontracting which will be covered in Chapters 9 and 10. If you plan to have a receptionist, that person will have to be on payroll by law; there is no option for contracting out this position. You will need to obtain copies of the regulations for subcontracting employees from your government.

2.6a Location and facilities

Describe the site of your business, the facilities (e.g., plumbing for sinks) that are presently in place, the facility (leasehold) improvements required or desired, and the features that make this an attractive site for your venture. If applicable, attach sketches and drawings of the layout and plan for the site.

Also include a description of the area where you will be setting up shop and why it is a suitable location for your business.

2.6b Equipment

Describe the necessary office, mechanical, operational, and transportational equipment that is required to run the business. Make a note if any of the equipment is already owned or needs to be acquired. If it is to be acquired, state whether it will be leased or purchased, and the costs involved in doing so.

2.7 Market research

Describe your target market; include demographic profiles, the geographic location, economic trends, and projection in the growth of the market. Research and include a market share analysis. Show how your business will affect the market and how much of that market you can reasonably capture. Indicate how you intend to capture this market share.

This section can be the most difficult part of your business plan. A good number that seems to work well with tattoo and piercings studios is one or two studios per every 20,000 people, any more than this and it becomes hard to make a living. Statistics on demographics can be obtained from your local government. These statistics are obtained from census polling and government departments that track public expenditures.

Traditional marketing strategy consists of three components, known as the "Three Cs":

- **Company:** Know the strengths and weaknesses of your studio.

- **Competition:** Know the strengths and weaknesses of your competitors.

- **Customers:** Know who your customers are and what they want.

You need to identify your direct and indirect rivals as well as gauge your potential fit in the marketplace. Direct competitors are commercial tattoo and piercing studios in your geographic area and indirect competitors would be home-based tattoo and piercing studios or studios that are not in your geographic area. Here are some issues to consider:

competitor strengths and weaknesses, whether new competitors are entering the marketplace, and whether existing ones are leaving.

2.8 Sales and marketing strategy

The next step is to develop a marketing strategy, which involves analyzing the "Four Ps," collectively known as the marketing mix:

- **Product:** What are you selling?
- **Price:** How much will you charge?
- **Place:** Where will you sell your product?
- **Promotion:** What special incentives will you use to get people to try your product?

To describe how you plan to promote your product and service you will need to answer the following questions:

- Do you plan to attend trade shows or place ads in trade magazines?
- Will you produce flyers to distribute to the public?
- Do you have any ideas for an advertising campaign?
- Do you have a plan in place to gain free publicity to create awareness about your product?

Determine a time line (i.e., in which months will these actions take place) and a budget for the first year of promotion. Sample 1 is an example of a cost analysis for advertising and promotion. If you would like to create your own, use the template (Promotions and Advertising) on the CD and make changes as necessary to fit your business.

Describe the method you will use for pricing your product or service. For example, will you accept credit cards, checks, and/or debit cards?

There are four pricing factors to consider for your services and products:

- What are the input costs? (Cost to offer the product.)
- What is the customer's perception of value? Is it high quality, medium, or low?
- What are your competitors charging?
- What are the expected profit margins?

These marketing and competitive analyses are vital parts of your business plan and will likely be the most extensive portion of it. Take the time to do thorough research on your competitors and how the market has behaved in recent years. A disorganized or unfocused marketing strategy can lead to disaster even for the best of companies.

2.9 Financial Plan

The financial plan is the section that determines whether or not your business will be financially viable. It will determine whether or not your business plan is going to attract any investment. The financial plan consists of three financial statements, the income statement, the cash-flow projection, the balance sheet, and a brief explanation of these three statements. The CD includes templates of the financial statements for your use.

Break the business expenses into two categories: your start-up expenses and your operating expenses. All the costs of getting your business up and running go into the start-up expenses category. These expenses may include: business registration, starting inventory (e.g., body jewelry), rent deposits, down payments on property, equipment purchases, utility deposits, furniture, and decor. This is just a small list of start-up expenses. There will be many more that you will add as you decide what you need.

All the costs of keeping your business running day to day are in the operating expenses category. Think of these as the things you're

Sample 1
Cost Analysis for Advertising and Promotions

Action/Advertising	Cost
Radio	$2,000
Newspaper	150
Brochures	250
Public Relations	250
Trade Show	1,000
Specialized Packaging	150
Internet	1,500
Yellow Pages listing	2,400
Total	**$7,700**

Month	Promotional Activities	Cost
Jan	Internet ($125) Yellow Pages ($200) Radio ($500)	$825
Feb	Internet ($125) Yellow Pages ($200) Radio ($500)	825
Mar	Internet ($125) Yellow Pages ($200) Radio ($500)	825
Apr	Internet ($125) Yellow Pages ($200) Radio ($500)	825
May	Internet ($125) Yellow Pages ($200) Trade Show ($1,000)	1,325
Jun	Internet ($125) Yellow Pages ($200) Newspaper ($150)	475
Jul	Internet ($125) Yellow Pages ($200) Brochures ($250)	575
Aug	Internet ($125) Yellow Pages ($200)	325
Sep	Internet ($125) Yellow Pages ($200) Public Relations ($250)	575
Oct	Internet ($125) Yellow Pages ($200)	325
Nov	Internet ($125) Yellow Pages ($200)	325
Dec	Internet ($125) Yellow Pages ($200) Specialized Packaging ($150)	475
	Total	**$7,700**

going to have to pay each month. Your list of operating expenses may include: salaries (i.e., your salary and staff salaries), rent, telephone and cell phone, utilities, medical supplies, inks and needles, advertising, and office supplies. Again, this is just a partial list to get you going. (See Chapter 7 for other supplies you may need.)

2.9a Income statement

Sample 2 is the income statement that you will need to include in the financial plan section of the business plan. The income statement shows your revenues, expenses, and profits for a particular time period. The CD includes an Income Statement template for your use.

Not all of the categories in this sample income statement will apply to your studio. For example, you might not sell any aftercare products, or you might only do tattoos and not piercings at your studio. Leave out those that don't apply and add categories where necessary.

2.9b Cash-flow projection

The cash-flow projection shows how cash is expected to flow in and out of your business. For you, it's an important tool for cash-flow management, letting you know when your expenditures are too high or when you might want to arrange short-term investments to deal with a cash-flow surplus. As part of your business plan, a cash-flow projection will give you a much better idea of how much capital investment your business idea needs.

For a bank loans officer, the cash-flow projection offers evidence that your business is a good credit risk and that there will be enough cash on hand to make your business a good candidate for a line of credit or short-term loan.

Do not confuse a cash-flow projection with a cash-flow statement. The cash-flow statement shows how cash has flowed in and out of your business. In other words, it describes the cash flow that has occurred in the past. The cash-flow projection shows the cash that is anticipated to be generated or expended over a chosen period of time in the future.

While both types of cash-flow reports are important business decision-making tools, we're only concerned with the cash-flow projection in the business plan. You will want to show cash-flow projections for each month over a one-year period as part of the financial plan portion of your business plan.

There are three parts to the cash-flow projection. The first part details your *cash revenues*. Enter your estimated sales figures for each month. Remember that these are cash revenues; you will only enter the sales that are collectible in cash during the specific month with which you are dealing.

The second part is your *cash disbursements*. Take the various expense categories from your ledger and list the cash expenditures you actually expect to pay for each month.

The third part of the cash-flow projection is the *reconciliation of cash revenues to cash disbursements*. As the word "reconciliation" suggests, this section starts with an opening balance, which is the carryover from the previous month's operations. The current month's revenues are added to this balance; the current month's disbursements are subtracted, and the adjusted cash-flow balance is carried over to the next month.

Sample 3 shows a cash-flow projection. There is a Cash-Flow Projection template on the CD that you can use for your business plan (and later on when your business is up and running).

Remember, the closing cash balance is carried over to the next month. The main danger

𝔖𝔞𝔪𝔭𝔩𝔢 2
𝔍𝔫𝔠𝔬𝔪𝔢 𝔖𝔱𝔞𝔱𝔢𝔪𝔢𝔫𝔱

Company Name:_____

Income Statement for the year ending 2011

REVENUE	
Service	
Tattoo room rent/commission	$84,000
Piercing room rent/commission	34,000
Total Service Revenue	**$118,000**
Sales	
Body jewelry	$30,000
Total Revenue (Service + Sales)	**$148,000**
EXPENSES	
Direct Costs	
Salary (Owner)	
Wages	
Unemployment insurance	
Employment taxes	$24,000
Mandatory government deductions (e.g. Federal Insurance Contributions Act, Canada Pension Plan)	
Workers' Compensation	1,500
Other:	
Total Direct Costs	**$25,500**
General and Administration	
Accounting and legal fees	$500
Advertising and promotion	7,700
Bank charges	250
Depreciation and amortization (on equipment and building if you own it)	250
Insurance	500
Decor	500
Office rent	24,000
Telephone	2,500
Utilities	2,500
Credit card charges	500
Medical and aftercare supplies	6,000
Tattoo ink, needles, and parts	6,000
Property tax	2,000
Security system	600
Equipment	5,000

Furniture and media equipment (e.g., TV, DVD player)	5,000
Renovations	2,000
Security system	
Other:	
Total General and Administration	**$65,800**
Total Expenses	**$91,300**
Net Income before Taxes	**$56,700**
Income Taxes	**$9,500**
Net Income	**$47,200**

SELF-COUNSEL PRESS — START & RUN A TATTOO & BODY PIERCING STUDIO/11

when putting together a cash-flow projection is being overly optimistic about your projected sales.

2.9c Balance sheet

The income statement only shows a portion of a business's financial picture. There are excellent profits being made, but what about its debt load? (Is the business holding too much debt in relation to its profit?) The other financial statements do not give a good enough view for a bank manager to see how solvent a company is (i.e., what ability the business has to liquidate its assets to potentially pay off its debts).

The balance sheet presents a picture of your business's net worth at a particular point in time. It summarizes all the financial data about your business, breaking that data into three categories: assets, liabilities, and equity. To create your own balance sheet, there is one similar to Sample 4 included on the CD.

At the end of your balance sheet, if *Assets = Liabilities + Equity*, then you've done it properly.

Once again, this template is an example of the different categories of assets and liabilities that may apply to your business. The balance sheet will reproduce the accounts you have set up in your general ledger. You may need to modify the categories in the balance sheet template provided on the CD to suit your own business.

Once you have your balance sheet completed, you're ready to write a brief analysis of each of the three financial statements. When you're writing these paragraphs, you want to keep them short and cover the highlights, rather than writing an in-depth analysis. The financial statements themselves (i.e., income statement, cash-flow projection, and balance sheet) will be placed in your business plan's appendixes.

2.9d Financing

Sample 5 includes some of the things that would go into preparing you for what you will spend on start-up costs. You will find a Start-up Costs template on the CD for your use.

Sample 3
Cash-Flow Projection

The following cash-flow projection is just a sample including only two months. The form on the CD is set up for 12 months.

	January	February
Cash Revenues		
Revenue from Product Sales	**$2,000**	**$3,000**
Revenue from Service Sales	**10,000**	**12,000**
Total Cash Revenues	**$12,000**	**$15,000**
Cash Disbursements		
Cash payments to trade suppliers	$1,000	$1,500
Management draws	2,000	2,000
Salaries and wages	0	0
Promotion expenses	500	500
Professional fees	500	500
Rent or mortgage payments	2,000	2,000
Insurance	100	100
Telecommunications	200	200
Utilities	200	200
Total Cash Disbursements	**$6,500**	**$7,000**
Reconciliation of Cash Flow		
Opening cash balance	$2,000	$7,500
Add total cash revenues	12,000	15,000
Deduct total cash disbursements	6,500	7,000
Closing Cash Balance	**$7,500**	**$15,500**

Sample 4
Balance Sheet

The following cash-flow projection is just a sample including only two months. The form on the CD is set up for 12 months.

(COMPANY NAME)	
Balance Sheet as of December 31, 2011	
ASSETS	
Current Assets	
Cash in bank	$40,000
Petty cash	1,500
Total Net Cash	**$41,500**
Inventory	$2,000
Accounts receivable	0
Prepaid insurance	500
Total Current Assets	**$44,000**
Fixed Assets	
Land	
Buildings	$20,000
Less depreciation	1,000
Net land and buildings	19,000
Equipment	
Less depreciation	
Net equipment	
Total Assets	**$63,000**
LIABILITIES	
Current Liabilities	
Accounts payable	$2,000
Vacation payable	0
Unemployment insurance	0
Mandatory government deductions (e.g., FICA, CPP)	500
Federal income tax payable	$9,000
Workers' Compensation	0
Pension payable	0
Union dues payable	0
Medical payable	0
State or provincial taxes payable	2,000
Taxes charged on sales	1,000
Taxes paid on purchases	2,000
Taxes owing	1,500
Total Current Liabilities	**$18,000**

SELF-COUNSEL PRESS — START & RUN A TATTOO & BODY PIERCING STUDIO/11

Long-Term Liabilities	
Long-term loans	5,000
Mortgage	0
Total Long-Term Liabilities	**$5,000**
Total Liabilities	**$23,000**
EQUITY	
Earnings	
Owner's equity — Capital	$10,000
Owner — Draws	24,000
Retained earnings	3,000
Current earnings	3,000
Total Equity	**$40,000**
Liabilities + Equity	**$63,000**

SELF-COUNSEL PRESS — START & RUN A TATTOO & BODY PIERCING STUDIO/11

2.10 𝔉orecasts and projections

Investors as well as yourself will find it helpful to see how you envision your company evolving and reacting to the ever-changing market. The questions you will need to address in this section include:

🌸 Does recent data show the market for your product/service is growing?

🌸 Do you have a plan to offer new products or line extensions in the first few years?

🌸 Are there other ways to position your company more competitively in the marketplace?

3. 𝔕evisit 𝔜our 𝔅usiness 𝔓lan

It is helpful to review your business plan at least every six months for the first two years, then after that once a year is sufficient. It shows how close your projections are and if you are keeping to your plan. It is not a bad thing to change the plan or adjust it (think of it as a work in progress). Just make sure what you change works with your original plan and does not conflict as this can cause problems.

Sample 5
Start-up Costs

Identify expenses to begin or expand business operations

Equipment	$10,000
Starting inventory	5,000
Advertising	2,000
Professional fees	2,000
Office supplies	500
Rent/mortgage	6,000
Land and/or buildings	0
Licenses	500
Telephone	500
Utilities	500
Repairs	1,500
Leasehold improvements	3,000
Vehicle expense	500
Deposits on utilities and phone	2,000
Other	_____
Other	_____
Other	_____
Other	_____
Total	**$34,000**

Sources of Capital

Where will the money for start-up expenses come from?

Owner investment	$10,000
Shareholders	
Loan monies	17,000
Lines of credit	7,000
Other	
Total	**$34,000**

SELF-COUNSEL PRESS — START & RUN A TATTOO & BODY PIERCING STUDIO/11

4

Setting up Your Business Structure and Finances

Starting a business can be an expensive endeavor, which can be intimidating because you have no guaranteed income from your business at first. Most new studio owners will be dealing with the situation of having to invest most or all of their savings as well as having to borrow money. However, if your business plan is solid, and you believe in your idea, you will achieve success. In this chapter we will discuss the various options for securing the finances to start up and run your studio, as well as the differences between business structures.

1. Setting up Your Business Structure

In order to figure out where to get the money you need to start your studio, you may first want to decide how you will structure your business. The types of business structures in the US include sole proprietorship, partnership, limited liability company (LLC), or C corporation. In Canada, you have the choice of creating a sole proprietorship, partnership, or incorporating your business.

The following sections give a general outline of these business structures. For more information you should discuss your options with someone who specializes in business start-ups, such as a lawyer, tax professional, and/or a business advisor.

1.1 Sole proprietorship

Setting up a sole proprietorship means you will be the only business owner. This type of structure involves the least amount of money, time, and paperwork to set up. If you don't have a lot of money for start-up, you may find this the easiest way to begin the business. As your business grows, you may eventually decide to incorporate. It is always a good idea to contact a lawyer and an accountant to discuss changing a business structure.

As a sole proprietor, you are completely in charge of your business. You will make all the business decisions without having to consult with a partner or board of directors. The benefit is that you will make all the profits from the business; however, the downside is that you will also be liable for all the debts that the business incurs. For tax purposes, you will be required to claim all of your profits or losses on your personal tax return.

The biggest disadvantage to being a sole proprietor is that your business will have unlimited liability, meaning you will personally assume all the risks and debts of your studio. This can make it difficult to acquire financing unless you have personal collateral (e.g., your house) to use as a guarantee in case you default on your loan.

The upside is that a sole proprietorship is very easy to set up. In the US, you are required to obtain a business license and seller's permit. You may have to acquire additional licenses from the state and/or city in which you will be operating your business. Check with the State Board of Equalization, Department of State, and City Hall for more information about filing documents and paying fees.

The State Board of Equalization collects state sales and use taxes. Use taxes are applied to consumer goods purchased without sales tax; for example, you purchased products from a vendor outside your state and it was delivered by mail or private courier, which means you have bypassed your state's sale's taxes. Some states require this use tax to be submitted yearly, while others expect it to be paid monthly. Check your local state laws in regards to use taxes as every state differs. You will also need to contact the Internal Revenue Service (IRS) about the forms you need to file for your business.

In Canada, as a sole proprietor, you will have minimal registration requirements. You will need to get a business license, and register your business name, as well as register for a GST or HST number. You will pay taxes by reporting income or losses on your personal income tax return. The income or losses will be part of your overall income for the year. Contact Canada Revenue Agency (CRA) for more information about business taxes.

1.2 Partnership

A partnership business structure means two or more people are owners of the business. This arrangement is similar to a sole proprietorship because of its ease of set up compared to incorporating. There are also the low start-up costs just like a sole proprietorship. If you and your partner expand the business, it is easy to convert a partnership into a different type of business structure, such as a corporation.

The two types of partnerships are *general* and *limited*. In a general partnership, the partners involved have the same amount of authority to manage and run the business. Instead of the business paying taxes, the partners are responsible for the taxes on their personal income taxes. The partners are also equally responsible for any debts the business incurs.

A limited partnership means one or more of the owners have elected to not have equal decision-making authority. With this structure, the partner with less authority has less or no responsibility for any debts the business may incur. If the partner has no decision-making authority, he or she is referred to as a silent partner.

It may be easier to acquire financing as a partnership as opposed to a sole proprietorship because you have two or more people that may be able to provide more collateral than one person. Another advantage to a partnership is that two people may have more start-up investment that can be pooled together to get the business up and running, which may mean you won't need to get loans from outside sources.

A partnership can also be good for sharing the workload with someone else. You and your partner can divide the work according to each person's strengths. This may be good in an area where one business partner is not licensed as a tattoo artist. (Note that some areas in North America require one of the owners to be a licensed tattoo artist. Check your government regulations and the local health authorities to see if this applies in your area.) For example, if you are more business savvy, you may take over the finances, while the other partner takes over the artistic side and takes care of hiring trained artists.

The biggest downside to a partnership is finding someone you can work with well. You may find that your partner is not doing his or her share of the work, which can mean you will take on more work than you originally signed on for just to make sure the business keeps operating. This can create resentment and snowball into bigger issues. You and your partner may end up spending more time arguing or trying to make compromises and less on making the business a success.

The setup for a partnership is similar to the sole proprietorship. In the US, you are required to obtain a business license and seller's permit (if you are selling merchandise and/or body jewelry). You may also have to acquire additional licenses from the state and/or city that you will be operating your business. Check with the Department of State and City Hall for more information about filing documents and paying fees. You will have to contact the State Board of Equalization because it collects state sales and use taxes. You will also need to contact the Internal Revenue Service (IRS) about what forms to file.

In Canada, just like a sole proprietorship, you will have minimal registration requirements. You will need to get a business license, register your business name, and register for a GST or HST number. You and your partner will include a share of the partnership income or loss on each of your personal income tax returns. The income or loss will be part of your overall income for the year. Contact Canada Revenue Agency (CRA) or go to the CRA's website for more information about business taxes.

1.2a Partnership agreement

It is highly recommended that if you are considering a partnership you should have a legal partnership agreement. A valid partnership agreement is written with the participation and agreement of all the partners and details how each partner is going to be involved in the business from start-up to its sale or dissolution. A partnership agreement helps prevent one or more partners being taken advantage of because the agreement spells out what each person's role is in the business. Note that some areas in North America require a partnership to have a written agreement.

The following topics should be covered in your written partnership agreement:

- ❀ Authority of each partner. For example, how much authority each partner has over the day-to-day operations, business decisions, and/or over the other partners.

- ❀ Participation. Outline the level of participation and duties of each partner such as how much money (including start-up investment and running the business), time, work, and what type of work each person is required to do.

- ❀ Division of profits and debts.

- ❀ Resolution of disputes. It is important to have the agreement explain how disputes will be resolved.

- ❀ Provisions for death, retirement, and succession.

- ❀ How dissolution of the partnership would work.

- ❀ Partner salaries, compensation, and benefits.

- ❀ Buyouts. For example, what if one of the partners decides to move and wants to get out of the business?

- ❀ Retaining the rights to business trademarks.

A partnership agreement must be written down and should be reviewed by a lawyer. After the agreement is made, and each partner is satisfied with what is described in the agreement, each person will sign and date the document. If you didn't have a business lawyer draw up the contract, then at least contact a lawyer and have him or her review it to make sure it is legal and binding. See *Partnership Agreement* published by Self-Counsel Press for more information on this type of agreement.

1.3 US limited liability company (LLC)

A limited liability company (LLC) in the US consists of one or more owners. Having an LLC means your company has limited liability from debt and, in some cases, lawsuits. You can also choose between being taxed like a corporation or like a sole proprietorship. If you don't want to incorporate, you can still have the freedom of limited liability from company debt.

Starting your company as an LLC does not always make it easier to get a lender unless you are willing to give a personal guarantee. This means that if you default on the loan, you are not covered under the limited liability of the company. Instead, what you put up as collateral, such as your house or car, will be used as such if you default on the loan.

The advantage of an LLC is that you and the other owners are protected from some liability for acts and debts of the company, but you are still responsible for any debts beyond the business's fiscal capacity. In most states, businesses are treated as entities separate from their owners. The downside is that many states levy a franchise tax or capital values tax on LLCs.

Note that starting your business as an LLC is more expensive that starting out as a sole proprietorship or partnership. If you are considering making your business an LLC, you will need to file Articles of Incorporation with your Department of State. The filing fees and tax fees vary from state to state. You will also need to create an Operating Agreement that details you and your partner's participation in the business. Talk to a business lawyer or business advisor who specializes in LLCs for more information on Operating Agreements. Check with your Secretary of State office for any other requirements for LLCs.

1.4 US C corporation

A C corporation is a business structure that exists legally as its own entity so that it may continue to run even if one of the owners is no longer with the corporation. Depending on where you live in the US, you may or may not need to have more than one person to form a corporation.

The owners of the C corporation are called shareholders (or stockholders). Shareholders are paid based on the percentage of shares or stocks they own in the company.

The advantage of this type of business structure is that the shareholders are not personally liable for any business debt. As a shareholder you can reap the benefits of the profits from the corporation without the liability of having to owe any personal money from any action of the corporation.

If this is your first business, you may find creating a corporation is more complicated and expensive than starting out as a sole proprietorship or partnership. For example, since no one is personally responsible for any business debts or corporate taxes, the corporation must deal with its own debt. The corporation must file and pay its own taxes. Each shareholder must also file and pay taxes on any money he or she receives as dividends from the corporate profits when filing his or her personal income taxes. This is considered double taxation because both the corporation and the shareholders are paying taxes.

Another disadvantage is that many people will be involved in the business, which can make things much more complicated. A board of directors will need to be elected and the board will make the executive decisions for the company. If any major changes are being made, the directors have to have their decisions approved by the shareholders. However, if you don't have start-up funds, you may need to consider this type of business structure. Getting investments from your shareholders may be the only way you can start your business.

Forming a corporation involves filing Articles of Incorporation with the Secretary of State, paying filing fees, and other fees as well as taxes. Talk to an attorney if you are considering making your business a C corporation. Note that starting a corporation also increases accounting fees.

1.5 Incorporation in Canada

Incorporating in Canada may be more complicated and expensive than starting your business as a sole proprietorship or partnership. If this is your first business start-up, you may want to start small; and when you eventually expand your business, you could incorporate it.

The biggest disadvantage to incorporating is the high start-up costs. You will also need to deal with other people such as shareholders, a board of directors, and officers. There are more documents to be filed, such as Articles of Incorporation, Annual returns, notices of any changes to the board of directors, and changes to the address of the registered office. As a corporation, your business will also need to maintain certain corporate records, and file corporate income tax returns. All of this increases accounting fees as well.

If you don't have a lot of money to start your company, incorporating your business may be a way to get investments from shareholders. Shareholders buy shares into the company and then they are paid based on the percentage of shares or stocks they own in the company.

The advantage to incorporating is that your company will have limited liability. This means that you are personally protected from lawsuits and creditors. If your company goes bankrupt, your personal property and finances should be safe, unless you have provided personal guarantees for your company's debt. This means that you and the shareholders will not lose more than your investments in the company. Also, creditors cannot sue you or the shareholders for debts incurred by the corporation.

If you are considering incorporating your studio, you should contact a business advisor or lawyer to help you set up the incorporation of your business properly.

2. How to Finance Your Studio

The best way to start a business is to be able to finance it yourself. Using your own money means you will have no lenders to account to, no bank interest to pay, and no debt hanging over your head as you are trying to get your business up and running profitably. You will need enough money to cover rent and upgrades for the studio, payment for enough equipment to get you started, registration fees and licenses, and advertising and publicity, as well as enough money left over to pay your employees. You will also need money that will last for at least six months to cover costs in your personal life such as mortgage or rent on your home, food, and other necessities.

The reality is very few in society are fortunate enough to start a business without some form of financial assistance. Unless you are one of the lucky ones who has a significant amount of money stashed away for your business, you will need to find ways to finance your tattoo and body piercing studio. There are various ways to go about getting money such as acquiring loans from financial institutions, personal lenders, and investors.

The first thing a potential lender will want to know is if your business is viable, so make sure your business plan is well prepared before you take it to the person or entity you are requesting a loan from. From a lender's perspective, they want to make sure they will be able to get their money back with interest.

There are many different ways to obtain financing for your business; it all comes down to what fits best with your situation and goals for your business. Just remember that any person or institution that lends you money will want to see that you yourself are contributing financially also from the start, so make sure that you have some money to invest personally.

2.1 Loans from financial institutions

Your first option is to try to get a loan from a bank or other type of financial lender. One thing a potential lender will want to know is your depth of understanding of the business. If you have a solid understanding of how to run a studio, and the ins and outs of the industry, your chance of getting a loan increases. The more experience you have, the more at ease the lender will be because it means you are more likely to succeed and the lender will get its money back.

If you have experience running a business, but don't have experience in running a tattoo and body piercing studio, you may want to consider partnering with someone who does have the related experience. This way you can show the lender that both you and your partner will have all aspects of the business covered. However, if a partnership is not something you are interested in then you might want to try working for another studio for a year or two to get the experience in the industry you need to prove to a lender that you are qualified to open this type of business.

If you have a bad personal credit history, chances are you will not be able to secure a loan from a bank or other professional lender. If you do find someone to lend to you even though your credit history is poor, your interest rates may be extremely high due to you being considered a risk. Contact the government-approved credit report agency in your area to see what your credit rating is and then go from there. If your credit history has any errors, you can contest the errors with the agency and possibly the creditor. If the history is bad due to your spending habits, then you will need to work on improving your credit such as paying off loans. You may also be able to work with the creditors to get them to remove the negative history from your file. Also check with the federal government to see if you can apply for business grants; there are programs for people with bad credit.

Most banks will make loans to businesses that already have an operating history, so you may find it difficult to find an institution that will give you a loan when you are first starting out. Many new businesses begin by using their primary savings as the initial investment into the business, which shows the bank that they are confident with your business idea by putting in their own money, not just wanting a loan to cover everything.

In order to get a secured loan from a bank or other financial institution, you may have to use your home or another significant investment as collateral. What this means is if you are unable to pay your loans, your assets are pledged to cover the costs if you default on the loan, or you may have to get a co-signer who has collateral.

The US Small Business Administration (SBA) is a good source for information on obtaining small-business loans. The Small Business Financing Program provided by Industry Canada can also help find information on securing a loan for your studio.

2.2 Personal lenders

Your second option is to borrow from personal lenders, which can include family or friends. The upside to this type of loan is that a personal lender may not require interest on the loan, which could save you a lot of money.

Usually a loan from family and friends is given in good faith, meaning no collateral is required. However, this comes with the downside of mixing business with personal relationships. If your business should go under before you can pay back the personal loans, the repercussions can include bitterness and estrangement from your loved ones. It is best, even with personal loans, to have a signed agreement drawn up by a lawyer to protect everyone's interests.

Another option is a relatively new concept of online personal lenders such as LendingClub or Prosper. Basically, these companies connect private lenders with borrowers. It saves you having to go through a bank with high interest rates. What you do is post the amount you want to borrow and the maximum amount of interest you are willing to pay. The potential lenders bid on the interest rate, which means the interest is lowered in the bidding war.

There is a personal element to online personal lending as well, which is you need to describe your situation and why you need the money. This provides investors with the information they need to know so they can decide whether to take a risk on you or not. Your situation is also based on credit scores and history, so if you have poor credit, your chances of getting a loan this way may not succeed. However, if you have a good credit history, this may be a way to save you and your business some money. Note that there is a fee that you will need to pay to the online providers.

3.3 Investors

Private investing can also be considered equity financing or venture capital. This happens when people put their money into your company in order to own a part or all of the business. You will need to be willing to give part of your decision-making powers to these outside investors, which may not be ideal for your situation, especially if you got into this to run your own business with no outside influences.

This type of financing is usually obtained by finding angel investors, venture capitalists, business partners, shareholders, or stockholders. If you do end up in this type of financing situation, you need to make sure everyone understands the amount of decision-making power each person has when it comes to the company. You may become stuck in a situation where you and the investors have different goals for the company, causing grief instead of success for your business. You will also be continuously paying the investors for their share no matter how much the business earns or expands.

If you decide to go this route, contact a good business lawyer to make sure you have sound agreements with any investors.

5
Creating the Business

There are many steps you will need to take before you open the doors to the public. You may want to make a list of all the things you need to get done. This chapter will help you make your list and guide you to setting up your studio properly.

1. Choosing Your Business Name

You have probably been considering different names for your studio since you decided to make your dream of owning your own business a reality. A name can make or break a business so make sure you don't take this decision lightly.

The most important thing to consider when naming your business is what you want the name to convey to your clients about your business and what it offers clients. The name should tell clients exactly what services you are providing. For example, you don't want your tattoo studio to be called "Hair of the Dog," because you may end up with people calling about dog grooming or hangover remedies! Jaded Body Arts is a good name for a tattoo shop because it is a catchy name; the word "Jaded" is unique, but the rest of the words tell what the business is about: "Body Arts" describes tattoos and piercings.

Make a list of names and then narrow the list down to your top five. Ask friends and family for their input. Having others give you feedback will tell you if the name is a winner or loser. Also watch for facial reactions because sometimes people try to be nice and not say what they are really thinking.

Consider the following when you are creating your business name:

- The name should be easy to spell and pronounce. If the name is easy to spell, then potential clients can easily look it up in the phone book or online. Also, do not use hyphens in your business name because hyphens are easily forgotten, and when clients are searching for you online, a missing hyphen may take them to a competitor's site.

- You want the business name to be easy to remember so that your clients will pass it along to others. Complex names are harder to remember. If your customers can't remember the name of the business, they won't be able to recommend it to other people.

- Don't choose a name that is part of a current fad or trend because it will go out of style quickly. If it's a pun, or funny now, it may not be in the future, or even understood.

- Keep your business name short. You want people to remember it and you want it to fit on a business card as well as on the sign outside your studio.

- Avoid abbreviations because they do not describe a business accurately.

- Make sure your business name is not close to any famous brand names. You don't want to be confused with other businesses while trying to build your own. Also, there are laws that prevent this kind of confusion, but they're usually

only enforced if the original owner of the name comes forward to complain. Regardless, you don't want to have to rebrand as you are opening due to name infringement because that means more money and time to redo advertising, signage, business cards, and so forth.

- Some business owners choose to use their own name for the business. For this type of business you may want to avoid using your name unless it sounds like a reference to body arts in some way. Also, if you decide to sell the business someday, having your name on the sign may be a deterrent for potential buyers.

- Since your business is for people who love art, your business name should be something with which you can create a nice design or logo, in essence branding your business. (See Chapter 8 for more information on branding.)

When you have narrowed down your list, search for the name on Google to make sure it is not used by others.

1.1 Filing a fictitious business name

If you are not using your legal name in the studio's name (e.g., Bob's Tattoo Shop), you will need to file a "fictitious" name at the local courthouse, county or state office, or government registry. The fictitious name is also referred to as assumed business name, operating as (o/a), trading as (t/a), trade styles, and doing business as (DBA).

In most states in the US, you will need to register your business name, except if you are a sole proprietor who chooses to use your own full legal name without any additional words added to it. However, if you are using a fictitious business name as a sole proprietor, you're in a partnership, or the business is a corporation, you will need to register the name. Depending on where you live, you will register either with the state government or the county clerk's office. Note that some states do not require registration of a business name.

Most businesses in Canada will need to register their business name, except for sole proprietors who choose to use their own name without any additional words added. (Note that in Newfoundland and Labrador, both partnerships and sole proprietorships do not have to register their names.)

If you are filing a fictitious business name in Canada as a sole proprietor, partnership, or corporation, you will need to begin by doing a business name search to make sure no one else is using that name in your area. When you have completed the name search you will file and pay the fees to register the business name at your corporate registry. If your business is a corporation, you will also need to prepare Articles of Incorporation, a cover letter, and complete an incorporation application.

In some areas of the US and Canada, you may be required to publish your fictitious business name in your local newspaper for a set period of time. The reason for this is to inform the public of your intent to operate under an assumed name.

Registering a fictitious name does not guarantee that another business will not use your exact name. The only way to ensure that no other business will use your company name is to register it as a trademark, or service mark the name, logos, or drawings that you would like to use for your business.

2. Seller's Permit

You will need to obtain a seller's permit if you are selling jewelry, clothing, or other products related to your business. In the US, you can get a seller's permit from the State Board of Equalization in your area. In Canada, the rules for a seller's permit differs in each province and territory. Contact the clerk at your local municipal government office for more information.

3. Employer Identification Number or Business Number

For payroll taxes to the Internal Revenue Service (IRS) and Canada Revenue Agency (CRA), you will need to acquire an Employer Identification Number (EIN) in the US, and in Canada, a Business Number (BN). This will be your business tax ID number. The EIN or BN assigned to your business will be used by the tax authorities to keep track of the amount of taxes you pay them.

You may also need to get a *State* Employer Identification Number from the state in which you are doing business, so that the state government can also keep track of the amount of state taxes you're paying. For more information about the state EIN, contact the Employment Development Department (EDD). The IRS and the EDD will provide you with information about paying your employee federal and state taxes.

In the US, you must file the applicable forms with the IRS to obtain an EIN. In the Resources section on the CD, there is a link to the IRS website that takes you to information about applying for an EIN.

In Canada, you must file the applicable forms with the CRA to obtain a BN. In the Resources section on the CD, there is a link to the CRA that will give you more information about applying for a BN.

4. Taxes

In regards to sales taxes, each state and province has their own rules. For more information, talk to the Internal Revenue Service (IRS) or the Canada Revenue Agency (CRA) about sales taxes and registration in your area. You can also talk to a tax accountant to help you figure out what is required for your business. Note that if you don't comply with your state, provincial, or territorial sales tax laws, you could end up with fines against your business.

You should also find out what forms you will need to file at tax time. In the US, you can get the forms from the IRS; and in Canada from the CRA. If you are not familiar with filing business taxes, it is highly recommended that you talk to an accountant who specializes in business taxes.

You may want to open a separate bank account to collect your sales tax so that it does not get mixed up with your other income (see section **5.**). This may make it easier for you when it comes time to submit the taxes to the IRS or CRA. Depending on your income, taxes collected will need to be sent to the government either monthly or quarterly.

Check with your local city business office to find out if you will need to pay any additional taxes for your business.

5. Open a Business Bank Account

You will need to open a business bank account, which is separate from your personal bank account. Mixing your business income with your personal savings almost always leads to mistakes in accounting; for example, you may not have as much as you thought in the account when you go to pay your taxes.

Research different banks to see which one will offer you the best deal for your business checking account. Some credit unions offer lower rates than commercial banks. When you are looking for a bank account, make sure you consider interest rates, fees for deposits and withdrawals, and the cost of ordering checks. Make sure you understand all the fees you will be charged before you sign up for an account. Those little charges can add up over time, and when starting a business you want to reduce costs wherever possible.

You may also want to ask if the bank has a special lineup for business owners. This way, if you have to make a quick run to the bank for change, you won't be stuck in the regular line waiting and wasting your time.

After you have established your business, you may want to consider getting a credit card for the business in case of emergencies. Your business computer may crash or equipment may break, and you might not always have cash on hand to replace the damaged or old items. Note some vendors only take credit cards for payment.

6. Insurance

Insurance may be one of the most important considerations for your business. There are many different types of insurance packages, so do your research and find the best insurance agent for your business. Make sure you, your business, and your employees are properly covered.

6.1 Body art and liability insurance

Your first step is to figure out what the insurance agents offer for plans in your area. You should look for agents that specialize in tattoo and body piercing policies. You want to make sure the insurance coverage you get will cover any situations that may arise.

Most likely you will need to get a *professional liability insurance* package. This type of insurance is similar to what doctors require to practice in certain areas of North America. The professional liability insurance protects your business from malpractice, negligence, and errors or omissions for body art. The coverage is mostly for legal defense costs in cases where a client is not happy with his or her tattoo or body piercing. Since art can be subjective, legal costs can rise quickly if a client decides to sue.

It may be hard to get insurance if your studio is a home-based business. Insurance companies like to provide services to businesses that are professional, legitimate, and permanently located in a building dedicated to the business. Home studios can be considered fly-by-night businesses, which means a risk for insurers.

The insurance company may also ask that you register your clients in a log to prove that you tattooed clients, along with the specific dates on which they were tattooed. This may be in addition to getting clients to sign liability waivers (discussed in Chapter 13).

Note that some insurance agents charge more for insuring studios that do facial and cosmetic tattooing (i.e., permanent lip color and eyebrows) because it is considered riskier than tattoos on the rest of the body.

6.2 Property and contents insurance

Property insurance is a necessity for your business because it protects the assets owned by the business, including the building and equipment, from destruction or damage. If you run your studio out of your home, you will need to get a separate policy from your homeowner's policy as a home policy will not cover your business equipment.

You will want to get insurance that protects your building and equipment from perils such as fire, flood, or theft. In order to determine how much property or content insurance you'll need, you should create a list of your business's assets and each asset's individual value. Once you have decided what assets you want to insure, and what their value is, your insurance agent can determine what your insurance payments will be. The reason you may not want to insure certain assets is because the items may not be worth the cost of the insurance premium. If you can't afford to replace the equipment, then you may want to insure it.

6.3 Disability insurance

As a business owner, especially if you are a sole proprietor, you should consider getting some type of disability insurance. For example, if you are hurt and will lose considerable business while you are recovering, or you're unable to carry on the business due to an injury, having coverage may save you from financial ruin.

7. Licenses and Certification

Every business that operates needs to get a business license. As for certification, that depends on where you live. Read on for more information.

7.1 Business license

You are required to obtain a business license. In the US, you can contact your local city office for information on how to obtain a license. In Canada, your local municipal business license office will issue it to you.

More than likely, you will have to display your business license up front where potential clients can see it. Your artists may also be required to display any licenses or certifications they have in their tattoo and piercing workstations.

In Canada you can do a quick search on the Canada Business website for what permits and licenses you may need for your business. A link to the site is included in the Resources section on the CD.

7.2 Artist certification

Depending on where you live, it is possible that individual artists don't need a license. Some places only require a studio to have certification, not the artists who work there. This is due to lack of regulations by the government for formal training of tattooists and piercers.

The Occupational Safety and Health Administration (OSHA) created a Bloodborne Pathogens Standard to help prevent those working in health care, tattoo, and body piercing industries from contacting bloodborne pathogens. That being said, some US states require artists to be certified in bloodborne pathogens using the OSHA standards. This type of training includes learning about managing infectious diseases in the workplace, learning how bloodborne pathogens are spread, and learning how to prevent exposure and what

you can do if you are exposed to infectious materials. For more information about courses, and before you sign up for a course, contact the Department of Health in your area. The Department of Health may have specific guidelines on where you or your artists can take the course to be legitimately certified. Note that in many states, yearly training is required in order to keep certification valid. You can also contact the American Red Cross for more information on bloodborne pathogens and the courses it offers.

Note that in Canada, training seminars that use OSHA's standards are provided by health educators. These educators have specifically tailored programs for the tattoo and body piercing industry.

Some tattoo conventions will offer courses on topics such as bloodborne pathogens, proper sterilization procedures, and other topics related to the art of tattooing and body piercing. These courses are generally more specific to the tattoo and piercing industry than bloodborne pathogen courses offered by other educators or institutions.

6
General Laws, Regulations, and Health Regulations for Tattoo Studios

There is very little consistency when it comes to laws and regulations for tattoo studios and their artists and piercers. Regulations differ from state to state and province to province. They also differ within each state and province by city, county, municipality, etc. Some cities don't even allow tattoo studios. In this day and age, it is hard to believe that some people are still so closed minded when it comes to body art and associate it with a "bad" crowd.

In order to make this book as comprehensive as possible, we gathered different regulations from around North America just so you would know what you are in store for when you are talking to the regulators in your area. This chapter by no means covers every law but it will give you an idea of some of the rules that may need to be followed in your area.

The Resources section on the CD includes a few websites that will point you to different laws around North America. New Jersey has some of the most detailed regulations online, so we have included a link to that government site as well. Also note that laws are constantly changing so you will need to be vigilant to stay on top of changes and always read what new laws and regulations are passing in your area. The Internet, your local government offices, and health authority can provide you with the regulations in your area.

1. Studio Regulations

There are many different studio regulations, and as said earlier, they differ in each jurisdiction. Here are some of the regulations we gathered that may or may not affect your business, depending on where you set up:

- You cannot open a studio within a certain radius of schools, churches, malls, or places where children play or hang out such as parks or playgrounds.

- Yearly and/or random inspections by the local health authority.

- A physician, osteopathic physician, or dentist must review and inspect artist techniques, equipment, and procedures. The physician or dentist must also provide semiannual training to the artists in regards to infection control, emergency procedures, and sterilization. (Note that Florida has this rule in place.)

- A physician must be at least a 50 percent owner of a studio.

- A tattoo artist has to be either 100 percent or 50 percent owner of the studio, meaning an untrained person such as a businessperson cannot open a studio.

- Spore testing is to be done weekly, monthly, or quarterly. (The Resources section on the CD includes a link to Autoclave Testing Services, Inc., which shows what each state requires for spore testing.)

- Clean workstations with a sink that includes hot and cold running water as well as a foot pedal must be present. The sink must be separate from a restroom.

- You need a working autoclave.

- Disposable needles must be used.

- You need a garbage container with a cover.

- You need adequate lighting and ventilation.

- The building must be in good repair.

- The restrooms must be clean and in good working order and available to clients.

- Storage cabinets must be present for tattoo supplies and equipment.

- Licenses must be displayed for clients to see in the front desk area and/or workstation area. You cannot display expired licenses.

2. Artist Regulations

There are many artist regulations put in place to protect the clients as well as the artists, which include the following:

- Artists cannot tattoo if they have communicable diseases including but not limited to tuberculosis, mumps, and chicken pox, to name a few.

- Smoking, food, and drinks are not allowed in the artists' workstation areas.

- Single-use disposable ink containers that are discarded after each use must be used.

- Artists must have certification and registration with some states or provinces where they are employed.

- Many areas require that artists take a yearly bloodborne pathogens course and display the course certificate in the front area of the studio or in their individual workstations.

- Artists must have a certain amount of hours of experience before they can be employed in the profession. For example, New Jersey law states that an artist must have at least 2,000 hours of experience.

- Artist must show an understanding of proper sanitation such as using gloves, washing hands, and sanitizing workstations.

- Tattooing services cannot be provided in a person's home or at a party or function because only a shop license applies for tattooing services within the shop.

- Some jurisdictions do not allow tattooing on the face, head, neck, hands, or wrist areas.

3. Regulations for Serving Clients

There are many regulations put in place to protect clients besides the ones mentioned above. This section is slightly more client specific.

Many areas require clients to be the age of majority or older and they must show valid government identification to the artist before being tattooed. However, some areas still allow teenagers younger than 18 to get a tattoo. In these instances, a parent or guardian must give written permission, sign consent forms, and be present while the child is getting tattooed or pierced. Many studios, regardless of government regulations, opt out of tattooing minors due to maturity levels and because the skin will stretch and ruin the tattoo as the child grows. If you are allowed to tattoo minors, you may be required to keep the minor clients' records for up to ten years. (For adult clients, the records are usually expected to be kept for at least two years.)

Piercing may be allowed without consent in some areas if a child is older than 16. However, it is always best to get consent for a child that has not reached the age of majority. If your jurisdiction allows piercing of minors, more than likely, a child younger than 16 will need a parent to sign a consent form and be present during the procedure. Note that genital and nipple piercings are not permitted for minors no matter whether or not a parent or guardian consents.

Other regulations to consider when dealing with clients include:

- The client must be sober.
- The client must be of sound mind.
- Aftercare instructions must be explained and provided in written form to the clients.
- Some jurisdictions do not allow artists to tattoo offensive or hateful words or images on clients. This may include gang symbols in areas where gangs are prevalent. You can check with local law authorities to see if there are gang symbols or offensive symbols that are commonly worn in your area, and if there are any laws against tattooing these symbols.

4. Other Rules

Cosmetic tattooing (e.g., eyebrows, eyes, or lips) is regulated differently than regular body tattooing. Most areas do not allow tattoo artists to do cosmetic tattooing. Cosmetic tattooing is considered a specialized area that only specially trained and licensed physicians can perform.

Some jurisdictions have rules and regulations on the types of sterilizers (autoclaves) that can be used in the studio. Some sterilizers that may be used in one state or province or even the same state or province but different city may not be allowed in your area.

Many studios like to partner with other professions such as massage therapists, hairdressers, and barbers, to name a few. However, not all jurisdictions allow tattoo studios to have other contractors or professionals working in the same studio as tattoo artists. This includes laser-tattoo removal.

Some states and provinces lack regulation so studios must take the necessary steps and precautions to protect themselves as well as their clients against diseases and inferior products such as tattoo ink and body jewelry. If a certain area lacks in regulations and it will cost you more to go above and beyond the regulation, spend the extra money as you have an ethical obligation to protect your clients from any physical impairment from your studio and its procedures and products. An area within the tattoo industry that is one of the most lacking in regulations is the wholesale and distribution of tattoo inks. Unfortunately, the government doesn't provide stringent regulations in this area, and it should. Some inks can contain harmful ingredients to humans such as certain metals and should be tested for amides, which have cancer-causing agents.

Also if a client has received a tattoo with ink that contained metals, he or she will not be able to have an MRI (Magnetic Resonance Imaging) because the metals react with the machine, causing pain to the person as well as a blurry picture. This could be a major health problem if the person ever requires an MRI. Another concern is laser therapy provided by some chiropractors; the laser heats up the metals in the tattoo ink causing the client to feel a painful burning sensation, and it may even damage the skin. Be sure to research what inks you and/or your tattoo artists are using at your studio, for the safety of your clients.

5. Health Inspections and Regulations

Generally, tattooing and body piercing is a somewhat self-regulated industry, meaning there isn't a standard set of government regulations in North America.

The US Health Department and Health Canada have rules that tattooists and piercers must follow, such as how to deal with the control and prevention of infection. Also, city health inspectors must inspect facilities yearly. If the health department receives complaints about a particular studio, they will check on it to see if it is following safe health procedures.

In North America studios are required to follow Occupational Safety and Health Administration's (OSHA) "Standard Precautions"; these are standard practices that must be adhered to by any workers that come into contact with bloodborne pathogens or Other Potentially Infectious Materials (OPIMs). Other than that, there are no consistent federal rules, laws, or regulations to govern the industry.

5.1 Health permit

In order to determine what health permits you need to establish your tattoo and body piercing business, you should contact your local Department of Health. You will receive a health permit for your business once the health department ensures that you have met the proper regulatory requirements in your area.

The health department will want to make sure your business does not contaminate clients with diseases such as hepatitis during the tattooing or piercing process. The health inspector will verify that your business properly uses, sterilizes, and stores the tattoo equipment. The inspector will also make sure your business abides by the health codes.

5.2 Spore testing

Spore testing is where you take a package that consists of thousands of living bacterial spores and put it through your autoclave. After you put it through the autoclave, you send it to an independent laboratory for testing. The lab will incubate the package and if there is something still alive, then your autoclave is not properly sterilizing your equipment. If you pass the spore test, you will receive a report by mail. However, if the test shows active bacteria, the lab will call you right away. Depending on where you live, you may have to do the spore testing weekly, monthly, or quarterly. (See the Resources section on the CD for tattoo autoclave spore-testing regulations in the United States.)

A spore-testing kit can be purchased from an independent lab that provides these services. Your autoclave provider should be able to recommend some labs that do this testing.

Some areas in North America don't have health-board regulations in regards to spore testing. However, if you reside in one of the areas where it is not mandatory, you should still do it. The reason is that your clients want to feel safe, and you want to make sure your clients are protected from diseases such as hepatitis, HIV, or tuberculosis to name a few. In order to prove you are a clean and safe studio, regular testing of your autoclave is important, and if your clients ask to see the test results, you can proudly show them. Some laboratories provide a certificate that you can display in your studio showing that you actively participate in a spore testing program.

7

Setting up Your Studio

In order to make your studio match your brand or just to make it fit with what clients expect, you may need to do renovations. You also need to make sure your signage is done well and put in place before you open your doors. There are many things you will need to have in place before you open, so this chapter will help you think about what you need to do to set up your studio.

1. Renovations

When deciding on a bay location it is important that you remember that tattoo and piercing studios must adhere to strict health-board regulations; health-board regulations required for tattoo and piercing studios vary from state to state and province to province so you must be aware of these before picking a bay. Being aware of these regulations before you buy or rent a space could save you thousands of dollars in renovation costs.

Some health-board regulations state that every workstation in the studio must include a sink with hot and cold running water, and a foot pedal for turning the water on and off. The studio floors must be easy to clean to prevent infection or contamination from biohazard material. This means no carpet or fabric floors or walls.

Plumbing can be expensive to set up in your new studio, so you may want to look for old hair salons, which make excellent studios because they usually have a lot of sinks. Hair salons also never have carpet and they are usually in good locations.

Pricing and estimating how much time renovation projects will take can be a tricky process with so many variables involved. A good idea is to always estimate higher on the costs and longer on the length of time to avoid frustration and lack of funds. You want to make sure your studio is ready for clients by the date you have advertised as the opening.

The fun part of renovating is designing the decor and choosing how to represent your business through the building it is in. Tattoo and piercing studios have a wide variety of styles to choose from, such as modern to classic, and trendy to campy, and everything in between. Continuity is important so whatever theme you choose be sure that it follows throughout the entire studio. Try to appeal to your clients and represent your business's brand; do not fall into the trap of picking only what you would like. With whatever style you decide to go with remember that cleanliness is important so the less clutter the better. For more information on branding your business, please refer to Chapter 8.

If your budget is tight, make sure to do any renovations that meet health-board requirements and state or provincial regulations. The fancy front desk or display art can wait until you start making a decent income.

2. Signage

Nothing screams fly-by-night business more than when someone puts up a handwritten temporary sign while waiting for a professional sign to be made. Signage takes a while to create, so you need to make sure you will have it up and ready before you open.

You will need to create the signage with a designer, wait for it to be made, and then make sure there are no typos or errors before you hang it. When you are negotiating with your sign provider, make sure you get a date in writing of when you will get the sign.

As a tattoo and piercing studio you can save money on design by designing the sign yourself or accessing your tattoo artists' talents; you will be able to create something very unique and appealing to the eye.

Signage is important as it is the clients' first impression of your studio. They will have already formed an opinion of your studio before even walking in the door, so make sure it looks good and is hanging up before you open; it will help create a buzz for your business.

There are many types of signs for the outside of your studio as well as large price differences. You will have to adhere to city regulations and your landlord or leasing company's requirements on size and design. Regulations can determine what type and design of sign you are allowed to erect so make sure to check these first before any decisions are made about what type of sign you want.

You will want your sign to weather the elements and blend in with neighboring businesses as well as grab your clients' attention. Signage allows potential clients to find your studio and attracts people walking by. Make sure the sign is big enough to be seen by street traffic as well as by people walking on the other side of the street.

As far as materials for signs, they range from wood to plastic to metal and neon. Neon is by far the most expensive and requires special wiring, with costs ranging from $5,000 to $20,000 per sign, but it is definitely eye catching. Plastic signs come in next in price and can range from

$2,000 to $5,000 without a lit background. Plastic signs with a lit background will cost anywhere from $5,000 to $15,000 per sign but have good durability and flexibility in design.

Metal signs have a nice industrial edge and expensive feel. Depending on which type of metal you choose it can cost anywhere from $2,500 to $5,000 per sign. Wood is the least expensive selection but it has the shortest longevity and will range from $500 to $2,500 per sign. (Note that these prices are approximate and based on sign dimensions of 8 feet by 4 feet.)

If you have the availability at your location for window lettering, it is an inexpensive and effective way to advertise your services and grab your client's attention.

A small indoor neon "open" sign is a great inexpensive way to grab customers' attention and let them know you are open. It is also important to list business hours on the door because if you are closed when your customers stop by, they will want to know when to come back. Sometimes a humorous or catchy phrase will bring clients back if you are closed when they stop by, because it gave them a laugh or caught their eye.

3. Payment Methods

How your business will receive payments from clients is up to you. Payment options vary from studio to studio with the common thread between them all being that no checks are accepted, ever. The majority of studios operate on a cash-only policy as the payment method. This is in part because most tattoo artists are independent or subcontractors and are used to being paid in cash daily. The positive of only accepting cash is you have the money instantaneously, and you save fees on debit and credit card machines and bank charges. Only accepting cash works well if your studio is smaller (e.g., one to three artists and piercers) so you are able to pay your artists daily if they like.

Most tattoo artists and piercers are currently used to being paid cash daily and switching this can be difficult. If you plan to have employees, rather than subcontractor services, keep in mind that switching to paychecks and waiting for debit and credit card deposits to become cash can be frustrating for the artists.

The standard in the past has been cash only for paying for tattoos and piercings in studios. This has been changing over the last five years due in part to how mainstream the tattoo and piercing industry has become. More studios are accepting debit and credit card payments now because of the demand from the public. Accepting methods other than cash can help decrease theft, and it can be a more effective cash-management technique. It can also increase your customer base because many clients like to have the option of using credit cards.

There are a couple of problems that arise with only taking cash and these are an increased chance of theft, internally and externally, because cash is easier and more tempting to steal than checks and or debit/credit card transactions, and it is harder to track for bookkeeping purposes. Some studios have ATMs (Automated Teller Machines) in them and receive a fee for each transaction run on that machine, allowing the clients the ease of getting cash and adding to the studio's profit.

For large tattoos that require more than one session to complete, it is recommended that payment is also divided between sessions. This way, the studio doesn't have to save the entire sum that was paid up front to pay the tattoo artist each session; and if the tattoo artist quits or leaves before the tattoo is finished the studio doesn't have to refund the money or pay more for another artist at the studio to finish it. Paying anyone up front before the work is done can be risky.

3.1 Credit and debit card machines

There are many different styles of credit and debit card machines. There are also many considerations such as cost of the machine, level of need for your business, and what credit card companies you will allow your clients to use for payment (i.e., Visa, MasterCard, American Express).

You may want to get a terminal with a printer that can process both credit cards and debit cards. These machines can range from $300 to $900.

Also consider whether you want the machine to be able to process multiple merchant accounts rather than just Visa or MasterCard. It may be beneficial for your machine to accept a variety of cards. However, this feature will cost you more.

Talk to your bank and do your research on the Internet to find out what the best machine is for your business. If you cannot set up a system through your bank, be vigilant with your research of the companies you are considering. Small-business associations can also help you find the best system to suit your business.

3.2 Payments to suppliers

Almost every supplier of medical, tattooing, and piercing supplies will only accept credit cards and COD (cash on delivery). COD is usually only accepted on orders less than $500. This basically means you must have a credit card to order supplies.

After being in business for at least a year or more, and proving to your suppliers that you are a reliable client, you may be able to discuss opening a vendor account. Basically the vendor allows you to buy on credit from it, but you have to pay your invoice by a certain date, which can be anywhere from 30 to 90 days. Make sure you pay your vendor accounts in a timely manner, because if you burn those bridges, you may lose vendors forever.

4. Equipment and Supplies

When choosing a company to purchase equipment and supplies from, remember that you have your clients' health in your hands, so be sure to order good quality items to protect yourself as well as your client. You also want your supplies and equipment to allow your artists to produce the best tattoos possible. There are numerous tattoo and piercing supply companies in the United States and Canada; all vary in price and quality. Nine times out of ten you really do get what you pay for.

Do not fall for it when new products claim fantastic, near impossible results. Make sure anything being offered to your clients has been researched thoroughly by the industry and by you.

You can usually purchase equipment wholesale by demonstrating that the equipment and supplies are needed for a commercial purpose. You may be able to negotiate a better price if you can secure a good sales representative to deal with on a regular basis.

You may be able to purchase secondhand equipment; however, this falls under the "buyer beware" category, and you should be aware of potential cross-contamination issues.

4.1 Medical equipment

Medical equipment you will need includes all the extra equipment used in tattoo procedures such as the following:

- Dental bibs
- Bandages
- Medical tape
- Drape cloths
- Disposable aprons
- Protective eyewear
- Iodine
- Disposable gloves
- Razors for hair removal

4.2 Tattoo equipment

You may not need to supply the tattoo equipment if you are in an area that requires artists to supply their own equipment. Note that most artists will have their own equipment, but you should inspect it to make sure it meets healthboard regulations for your area. Tattoo equipment includes:

- Tattoo machine
- Power supply
- Clip cords
- Needles
- Ink
- Tattoo chair and/or bed
- Tubes
- Grips
- Stems
- Machine parts

4.3 Piercing equipment

Piercing equipment includes:

- Needles
- Piercing tools

- Jewelry
- Gentian violet (used for marking the place of piercings)

There is great variance in body jewelry. You will need to look for good quality metal so make sure you are piercing with no less than surgical grade stainless steel 316LVM or Titanium Grade 2 with no alloys. Lower grade metals will result in allergic reactions to the client and longer healing time if the piercing heals at all. See section **5.** for more information on jewelry.

4.4 Sterilization equipment

Sterilization equipment includes the sterilization machines which are called autoclaves, chemiclaves, or steam-claves. Top-of-the-line machines kill every known virus and bacteria put through them and are the same units hospitals use to sterilize medical tools after surgery, before use on the next patient. They are capable of killing all forms of microorganisms, including protozoa, bacteria, fungi, algae, and viruses. Autoclaves can even penetrate the microbial spores that are resistant against all other forms of sterilizing agents and eliminate them.

How much money you will require to purchase these really depends on the quality of equipment you pick. Also, how many tattoo artists and piercers you have in your studio will change the amount of money required due to needing more machines.

You will also need to purchase disinfecting solutions for surfaces and sterilization pouches.

4.5 Calculating your equipment budget

You will need to figure out how much money to budget for equipment. The following amounts in this example are calculated using one tattoo artist and one piercer to give you an estimate on your total equipment budget:

- 🌹 Medical equipment: $2,000 to $3,500
- 🌹 Tattoo equipment: $2,000 to $7,000
- 🌹 Piercing equipment with jewelry: $2,500 to $8,000
- 🌹 Sterilization machine: $2,500 to $10,000
- 🌹 Other sterilization equipment: $500 to $1,000

You will require a minimum of $10,000 to $30,000 for equipment. Keep in mind if you are *not* the tattooist or piercer, the person you hire must supply his or her own equipment to operate as a contracted employee, according to government regulations in some areas. Check with the federal government for a complete listing of subcontractor requirements. If you hire your artists as employees, you will have to supply all materials required to perform procedures.

A recent development is the invention of completely disposable equipment for tattoos and piercings, eliminating the need for a sterilization machine. Contact your local health authority for more specific information in regards to health-board approved equipment.

4.6 Pigments and inks

One of the most important aspects to running a high-quality studio is to know intimately what products are going to be used on your clients. As the studio owner you should be knowledgeable on all products to be used in a tattoo or piercing, from start to finish.

As tattoos are the more permanent of procedures offered at any studio, the ink that is going into each piece should be of the highest quality to guarantee the best possible finished product. Cheaper is never better in this industry. You will get exactly what you pay for as not all inks are created equal.

Top-quality pigment or ink companies should be able to back up their products with ingredient listing and safety certification of some form. Both allow you to ensure the clients are receiving a tattoo free from heavy metals or known carcinogens. Be leery of companies who keep the basics, such as ingredients, a secret.

4.6a The three- to five-year tattoo ink myth

Be aware of mythical products that claim to do the impossible. A tattoo is a tattoo! It is permanent by nature. The fact is, when you insert tattoo ink under the skin, it's there to stay. It may fade over time, but it won't just disappear. There is no magical ink that fades completely away after a predetermined length of time.

Be very cautious with products that claim glow in the dark or UV reactive capabilities as well. These inks are no more temporary than traditional pigments, and have undergone less testing.

Some artists have claimed that they tattoo the ink so lightly that it doesn't become permanent — that somehow it's only embedded in a temporary layer of skin that will eventually wash away. This is impossible. There are three main layers of epidermis, and most tattoos go into the second layer. If you only go into the first layer what you'd be left with is a really crappy half-tattoo with splotches of ink here and there. The end result would not be temporary; it would be a poorly done piece of artwork.

4.7 Bandages

Proper bandaging is an important first step to heal a new tattoo. Various types of bandages are used within the industry for protecting a freshly applied tattoo. Options commonly used range from paper towel and plastic wrap, to liquid bandages, to Dry-lock bandages. Keep in mind that not all of these methods follow Occupational Safety and Health Administration's (OSHA's) Standard Precautions in the United States or Canada. In both countries these are specific to the personal service industry. Do your research, and become educated. You will be amazed at the controversies surrounding proper bandaging techniques.

Many experienced artists already have a preferred way of bandaging tattoos so discuss what their preferences are. Some artists are open to change and some believe in what they know. You would be surprised at the discussions I have had to endure regarding something as simple as bandaging. At this point I still have artists who do not use the same method; however, all of them follow OSHA's Standard Precautions to best protect themselves and their artwork, so more than one type of bandage is always on hand. It would be up to you as the owner to know which methods are being used by your artists and to ensure artists are following the expectations of your local health authority.

Be aware that products such as bandages can change in manufacturing or become obsolete. It is a good idea to stay on top of current changes, so that you can stock up if necessary when you find a method you really like.

4.8 Office equipment, furniture, and supplies

Do not forget to budget into your equipment and supplies what you will need for office use. You will definitely need a computer for your website upgrades, for customers to contact you by email, and you might even use it for all your scheduling needs. You will also need an external hard drive or another way to back up documents.

You will need a decent photocopier or a printer with good scanning capabilities in order to make copies of clients' photos or pictures (this way you can copy the pictures and return them to the client right away to prevent loss or misplacing of photos or pictures).

You will need decent chairs or stools for the artists to sit on while doing their work as well as a chair for the front desk person. Your waiting area will need chairs or couches for your clients to sit on while waiting. You should invest in a nice solid coffee table and/or end tables that are used to display the artists' and piercers' portfolios.

You may also need a display case for displaying merchandise and body jewelry.

Other items you will need include:

- Paper for drawings and paper for the printer
- Plenty of ink cartridges
- Stencil paper
- Drawing supplies such as markers, pens, pencils, etc.
- Desk-based scheduling calendar if you are not using a computer program.
- Filing cabinets for storing client information such as permission forms and business information.
- A telephone system that allows multiple lines so that your clients never receive a busy signal. Also, an answering service or machine that can take information when the studio is closed.
- Media equipment such as a stereo and good speakers and/or TV for the waiting room area.

A good security system is also recommended to keep your studio protected during the hours you are closed. Ask around for the best companies and pricing in your area.

5. Jewelry

There are many different styles and qualities of jewelry available on the market to be used in professional piercings. When first starting out focus on the basics such as standard jewelry that will be used most often for the majority of piercing procedures.

Research what the most common or popular piercings are for your area. Rely on your piercing staff to help guide your purchasing decisions. For body jewelry to pierce with you must order a metal quality of surgical stainless steel 316LVM or Titanium Grade 2 with no alloys, if you do not want to risk clients having allergic reactions. Also, if you don't have high-quality jewelry, the piercing will not heal properly, if ever.

There are surgical implantation grade plastics used for surface piercings and high motion areas, for clients involved in sports and for the one percent of the population that is allergic to surgical stainless steel 316LVM. This implantation plastic is good for healed oral piercings as it helps in avoiding gum recession or tooth damage sometimes caused by metal jewelry. As you can see, the knowledge base required by piercers is quite extensive, so never take training lightly.

Being aware of the difference in quality of jewelry, and using only the best, can ensure a positive reputation with your clientele. Body jewelry is like clothing, meaning one size does not fit all. It is recommended to start with a selection of various gauges and lengths, in all the basic styles.

6. Temperature and Lighting

You will want the temperature in your studio to be in a moderate range, meaning not too hot or too cold; around 70 degrees Fahrenheit or 21 degrees Celsius is preferable.

If your building has no air conditioning, you may wish to purchase portable units for the tattoo and piercing rooms because too hot a temperature can cause your clients to faint when receiving a tattoo or piercing, which can result in a myriad of problems. If the temperature is too cold, it can cause clients to shiver making the job of tattooing or piercing them extremely difficult.

Good lighting is of great importance so invest in the best lighting system you can find. Tattooing and piercing requires precision and attention to detail so good lighting is a must.

8

Marketing and Advertising

In order to get your business noticed, you need get people talking about it. Marketing and advertising your business doesn't automatically start after you open your studio doors. You need to get the buzz going before you open. This way you will have customers right from the beginning.

1. Pricing Your Products and Services

It is highly recommended that you set your prices within range of your competitors in order to avoid price wars. Price wars lower your profits in the long run and the competition will be more established and able to weather a price war better than you.

In pricing tattoos there are three methods, the most common is by the hour and will usually range between $100 to $200 or more per hour depending on the state or province, city, location within the city, and the quality of artists at the studio.

The second method of pricing is by the piece in which case the artists states a price for the tattoo regardless of the time it takes to finish, usually this price will fall into the $100 to $200 per hour range.

The third pricing strategy, and most rarely used, is the grid system. A grid is placed over the tattoo with each square costing a certain amount, usually within the $20 to $40 per square range.

For the pricing of piercings there are a couple different methods. One includes a set price for everything such as the piercing procedure, the jewelry, and aftercare products. Piercings with everything will range in price from $30 to $140 per piercing, again depending on the location and style of studio. The other method is to price everything separately, allowing the client to upgrade jewelry for a price and purchase aftercare products for another cost.

2. Branding Your Business

After you have decided on a business name, your next step is to brand your business. Branding creates a public personality for your business. Your brand gives potential clients a perception of your studio, so you need to decide how you want people to think of your business. Who do you want your target market to be? Do you have all female artists in your studio? If so, you may want to cater to an upscale market of women clientele.

Will you have popular guest artists from around the world in your studio? If so, will you market to the people who want the prestige of being inked by a famous artist in the tattoo community?

You want your brand to show what makes you unique and different from your competitors. The brand is your business's image so you should make sure it matches what your customers perceive your business to be. For example, if you are marketing to women, then you want to make sure your studio is designed for this type of clientele. When these clients walk in the door, they want to see brighter colors and art on the walls instead of dark walls and posters of rock stars.

Branding is about image, so make sure your image matches your branding of your studio, your artists, and advertising.

3. Business Cards and Flyers

A few weeks before you open, you should have business cards designed and professionally printed. You can then hand the cards out to everyone you meet that may be interested in getting pierced or tattooed. This will help your business begin with bookings from day one. This also means that you should have someone to answer your business phone before you open in order to start booking appointments.

You should design a logo to put on your business cards. This way people will come to recognize your brand. Basically, your business card with its logo reinforces your brand with potential clients.

Being that you are in an industry that is all about art, your business card and logo should be creative. A boring business card will hinder your business. That said, your business card should not be overly busy with text. It should include no more text than your business name and address, phone number, email, and website address.

To make the card less busy, a phone number and website address along with the logo and name of your business should be enough information to get people in the door. However, if you go this route, make sure you have a fantastic website that tells people about your business and where to find it.

You may also want to get some personalized business cards made for your artists to give out. Having their names on the cards will build a clientele for them as well as the studio.

If you are going to print flyers for your business, include the same contact information as your business cards. You may also want to include an incentive such as a discount coupon for those that book an appointment before you open.

You can hang fliers in places such as bars, coffee shops, and other businesses in the area that will allow fliers to be posted.

4. Creating a Buzz Online

There are many ways to promote your business online. Using social networking sites such as Facebook, MySpace, and Twitter is a great way to get free advertising. You can also create a blog that shows your knowledge of the industry. Of course, you must invest in a great website, which doesn't have to be expensive, but it is a necessity.

4.1 Social media

As soon as you have your business name, location, and an opening date set, start promoting your business. Again, using social networking sites such as Facebook, MySpace, and Twitter can be an inexpensive way to advertise that you are about to open to a wide population. The key for these sites to work as free advertising is to make sure you update your accounts often with fun, relevant, and new information. You want viewers to keep coming back for more information, which keeps your business in the forefront of the viewers' minds, meaning potential business.

Create a buzz for your business by making your Facebook Fan page interesting and fun. Update your status often on the progress of the business opening. Invite friends and family and encourage your friends to invite their friends to visit and comment on the page. Include pictures of the freshly painted and designed studio as well.

Post pictures of the artists' work so that potential clients can become familiar with your artists. Create separate portfolio picture albums for each artist to showcase his or her work. You can also post pictures of your licenses, health-board certification, and other important info to show clients you are taking every precaution to protect them by providing a clean and safe environment. If you have merchandise such as jewelry or T-shirts, add pictures of these items.

If you use Twitter, make sure you update your tweets often. If you don't have a lot of updates about the business or pictures to post of artists' work, then at least post interesting stats or news related to the tattoo and piercing industry.

Whatever you post, make sure it is relevant to your business and is not personal, such as "I walked my dog today." Use social media outlets to promote your business and gather clients. Remember to point people to your website as well.

4.2 Blogging

If you or one of your artists likes to write, create a blog (just like with social media sites, your blog should be about the business and not be personal).

You may want to discuss new advances in the industry, or new laws and regulations. You could write a weekly column on interesting facts and stories about the history of tattooing and body piercing. The point is to include anything that could be useful to your readers. If you are just writing to say, "We have a sale on jewelry," your blog becomes an obvious advertisement. However, if you show some pictures of the new jewelry and then go on to talk about the history of body piercing and how jewelry has evolved or improved over the years, your readers will become more interested.

When you hire new artists, introduce them on your blog with pictures of their work and a brief history of where they have worked or what great accomplishments they have done.

You can even include a picture of the artists if they are willing to have their pictures posted on the blog.

The secret to a good blog is to provide interesting information such as current events, relevant links, and new ideas to readers that will keep them coming back to read more. Do not cram sales down your readers' throats. You want to show your readers that you are someone who knows the industry; someone they can trust, which encourages them to become clients.

In order to gain followers and keep readers coming back to your blog, make sure you set aside time each week to update it. It takes time to gather information and write the blog, so schedule time for this. The blogging community likes consistency, so if you sporadically show up with a blog post once every few weeks or months, you will lose followers.

The posts don't have to be long, just informative. Include links to your Facebook Fan page, MySpace, and Twitter accounts so that readers can follow your more frequent updates on those sites. Also include a link to your website if your blog is not a part of your website.

4.3 Website

Having a website that is updated regularly is a must for any business nowadays. Before consumers will buy anything, they research what is out there usually by looking first at a business's website. Before you open your studio, you should have your website up and running.

Your potential clients want information about your business so your website should include where you are located, your contact info (i.e., email address and phone number), and hours of operation. This information should be on your home page, or at the very least, a highly visible link to this information. Clients don't want to search for it. If you bury this information, people will get frustrated and find another tattoo studio that does provide the information up front on its website. You may want to include your contact info at the bottom of every web page as well.

On your site you will want to include a page on your safety standards and practices, such as showing that you are certified to tattoo and body pierce in your area. Also, if the health board has approved your facility, include that information. If you do spore testing, that should be noted as well and explained so that consumers understand what spore testing is and why it is important.

You can have pages dedicated to your artists' work and mini-bios about them. Post great photos of the studio itself to show potential clients that your place is a comfortable place to get a tattoo or piercing.

You may also want to include a "news" page that has information about your business that has been published in magazines or newspapers. If your business contributes to causes in the community, that information can be added to your news page as well.

Having your blog linked or as part of the site is also helpful to get readers to return to your site often to read what you have to say. The more you have people come back to your site, the more chance they will want to come into your studio to be inked or pierced. It keeps your studio in clients' minds.

Ask clients if they would like to give comments that can be posted to a testimonials page. Make sure you update it occasionally to give readers who return to the site new information to read. If you decide to do a testimonials page, make sure you get your clients' permission before posting their names and comments.

You can also include a merchandise page, especially if you sell T-shirts or other merchandise that promotes your studio. You may also want to have a page that showcases the jewelry you have in stock or information about new merchandise that is coming in soon to your studio.

When creating your website, the most important thing to remember is that it should look professional and not like it was created from a template from the '90s. Every part of your business should look well-kept to keep up your image of a good business. The following tips will help you keep your site's image clean and professional:

- Do not clutter the website with too much information. Web readers want to find information easily so include lots of white space and short sentences and paragraphs.

- Get to the point and make the information clear. Use the active voice when writing text.

- Show good pictures and not fuzzy or poorly taken pictures. The pictures you include should be the best of the artists' work and the best of the studio. You want your potential clients to never doubt your studio is the *best* place to go for a tattoo or piercing.

- Every page should have value for your readers. Whether it is about looking for the right artist, what merchandise your studio offers, or an informative blog post on the direction of the industry, make every word and picture count.

- Do not annoy the viewers. This means do not include pop-up windows, blinking images or text, or gaudy backgrounds. While we are on the topic of annoying,

make sure your webpages load quickly for viewers. Nothing turns a viewer off more than a slow website. For pictures to load faster, use file compression graphic software so your pictures show up quickly instead of at a snail's pace.

- Make sure every page has a link to your homepage and contact information. Even better, every page should have a menu with links to all the pages you offer visitors so that they don't have to search for what they might have found interesting earlier in their search.

- The font should be in black on a white or cream-colored background to ease visitors' readability. Having red font on a blue background or white text on a black background is hard to read and can annoy viewers.

- The font size should be in the 12- to 13-point range. The easier the text is to read, the more chance visitors will stick around to see what you have to say and show them.

- Do not use all capital letters when creating text for your site. It looks amateurish and like you're yelling at readers. If you want to make something stand out, use bold or italics; however, use these sparingly. If you overuse these, it takes away from the points you are trying to make.

- Most important, make sure you use spell check. In addition to that, have a couple of friends or family members view your site before you post it online. Take their suggestions and learn from them.

If you don't know how to create a great website, invest in hiring a professional. The better your site looks, the more clients you will gain from it.

Another important tip is to make sure your website is updated regularly. Keeping it fresh with new blog entries or pictures will keep visitors returning to it and coming through your studio doors. If a website is out of date, it sets a bad example that tells viewers that maybe you don't keep your studio up to date either.

5. Ways to Advertise Your Studio

There are many ways to advertise your studio. Some are expensive and others are free. The important thing to remember is to always track your advertising to find what type of advertising is bringing in the most business. The best way to track it is by asking your clients how they heard about your business.

If you find that most of your clients come from other client referrals or by reading your website, but that only one or two came in due to newspaper advertisements, maybe it is time to drop the expensive newspaper advertising and focus on your stronger advertising venues. For example, if you find you are getting a lot of client referrals, what you could do is offer a 5 or 10 percent discount to those that have referred five clients who have booked appointments.

The following sections will give you some more ideas on how to advertise effectively.

5.1 Advertising through community and charity events

An inexpensive way to appeal to a target market is to get involved with your community and local charities. People love feel-good stories and so does the media, especially when it comes to reporting local events.

In Aiden Livingston's book *The Secrets of Advertising to Gen Y Consumers* (Self-Counsel Press),

he says, "I believe that every company should have some social outreach program and that they should publicize it incessantly … The company gets more business because Gen Y consumers appreciate its work to make the world a better place, and many worthy charities and causes get the funds and resources necessary to carry out their work. Furthermore, the donations made to many nonprofit organizations can be written off on the business's income taxes. When you consider all the benefits, such as free publicity, it is amazing that few companies have social outreach programs."

Find a cause that your business would be a good fit with and sponsor them. The charity will usually run newspaper and radio ads and have banners at the events displaying the names of the sponsors. When you pass out flyers for the charity event or the event is advertised in the news, your business name will be promoted as one of the sponsors.

You may also be able to meet potential clients at the event. Just don't push the sales, because the event is first and foremost about the charity being promoted. Having the studio's name connected with a good cause will increase public awareness of your business.

You may also want to donate merchandise such as gift certificates or clothing with your business logo on it, if the charity event is having contests or draws for attendees.

When your business is financially secure, say after the first couple of years, you may want to sponsor a local adult softball team or some other sports team. You can sponsor a local athletic team by donating money for the entry fee into the sport, and get advertising by providing the uniform T-shirts with your business's name on them.

There are many creative ways to get your name out into the community, so consider what is out there and what would be the best fit for your business. Becoming known in the community as a business that cares is always good advertising.

5.2 Co-advertise with other businesses

Introduce yourself to others businesses in the area. Getting to know your neighbors and the community can help build good will. Because of the negative view of tattoo studios that some people still hold, some businesses may find having a tattoo studio moving into their neighborhood will cause problems. Reassure those businesses by introducing yourself and inviting the owners to come see your studio. You may find that once they have seen the studio they will be less inclined to badmouth your business. You might even get some of them to be your customers.

Making friends in the community means you may be able to find other businesses to partner with when it comes to advertising. Maybe there is a massage therapy business down the street that will agree to recommend your services and you will recommend theirs. You and the other business may decide to share advertising space in the local newspaper or link to each other's businesses on each of your websites. Showing that your studio is accepted by other businesses in the area will show potential clients that you are a permanent part of the community and not a fly-by-night operation.

The biggest advantage to co-advertising, besides referrals, is sharing advertising costs. Some of the businesses you may consider co-advertising with are massage therapists, retail stores, and almost anything in the arts community.

5.3 Client referrals and word-of-mouth advertising

Your studio's first few clients are some of the most important clients you will ever have. Every customer that comes through the doors should be treated well, but the first satisfied clients are the ones that will start the ball rolling when it comes to spreading the word about what a great studio you are operating.

You may find that once you open the doors to your studio the easiest way to get clients is through referrals or word-of-mouth advertising. Nothing sells a business's services better than having happy clients.

You need to start building a clientele quickly in order to make sure your studio stays in business. You may want to give incentives to the first customers by offering them discounts if they recommend five or more clients to your studio. You may even want to give these clients some free merchandise such as T-shirts or hats or bumper stickers to help you spread the word that your business is open and ready to serve the public at large.

You want to gain repeat business as well as new business, so make sure every client is treated well. Every satisfied customer will show off his or her ink or piercings, which will be your best form of advertising.

5.4 Advertising in newspapers and magazines

It can be extremely expensive to advertise in newspapers and magazines, and sometimes not worth the money. If there is a local arts and entertainment magazine, that may be a good place to hit your target market.

If you do decide to advertise in a local newspaper or magazine, make sure you include the following in your ad:

🌹 Studio information such as the name, address, telephone number, and website URL. This may seem obvious, but sometimes the most important information is forgotten when people create ads.

🌹 Logo or slogan.

🌹 Information about the services and merchandise you sell. If you have something that makes your business stand out from your competitors, make sure you emphasize that unique feature.

🌹 Entice the readers by offering a deal or free gift if they come in to your studio with the newspaper clipping. This way you can also track how many clients you are acquiring from this type of advertising. If you aren't getting very many clients this way, you may want to look into other sources of less expensive advertising. Also, if you are offering a deal, make sure there is an expiration date so that you are getting client bookings right away.

The trick to a good newspaper or magazine advertisement is to draw in the reader. Give them a teaser of information, but enough information to get them into your studio. You don't want your ad bogged down with too much text, but you want to make sure it gives the readers everything they need to know to contact you.

When you are dealing with advertising salespeople, make sure you know what you want and that you don't get talked into an expensive advertisement that you didn't provide for in your budget. Listen to what they have to say as they may have some good tips on how to create your ad to better target your market. However, note that they are trying to make a living by selling ad space so make sure you stick to your advertising budget.

A way of getting free advertising from newspapers or local magazines is to either volunteer to write a regular column on current events or health-related aspects of the industry, or get a contact at the news source to write information about your business.

A good place to secure a weekly column may be in your local community paper or arts and entertainment magazine. If you do get a column, be prepared to write at least 500 to 1,000 words each week or month on information about the industry that is interesting and important to your target market. For example, what new regulations have been released in the health industry about body modifications? What new types of inks are being used such as black light tattooing? At the end of every column, include your name, your business's name, and contact info (i.e., website URL, email address, and/or phone number).

If you can't get a column, you may be able to get a local writer to write about events you are participating in, for example, if you are sponsoring a charity event or local sports team. If you are involved in speaking to students in high schools about safe tattooing and body piercing procedures, a reporter may be interested in covering that story. The key is to find something interesting that a newsperson will want to write about and share with his or her readers.

5.5 Speaking engagements

If you can become an expert about your industry, you may be able to secure some speaking engagements explaining safety procedures and other pertinent information to the community. Get involved with the local health authority and offer to speak at schools. Educating people about the industry and how to find safe and clean tattooing and body piercing studios will help increase your business as well as teach people what they should know before they get inked or pierced.

5.6 Newsletters

Besides keeping your clients updated on social media sites, you may also want to send email newsletters. Your newsletters may include industry info or what's new with your business. If you've added a new artist, you could write a bio about the new person and invite clients to book an appointment. If your business is involved in a charitable event, the cause could be discussed (make sure you include the date and time of the event).

In order to create a newsletter emailing list, you will need to collect email addresses from your clients. When they are filling out their permission forms before getting a tattoo or piercing, you could ask on the form whether or not they would like to receive newsletters by email. If so, they can include their email address on the form.

Another way to invite people to your emailing list is to have a sign-up section on your website that explains the newsletter and how often it is sent out to readers.

A newsletter should not be sent out more than once a month. Any more than that and it will become annoying to your clients. The newsletter doesn't need to be more than a page of information, and sometimes it can be less.

You don't want the newsletter to look like it's a sales letter; what you are creating is a more subtle advertisement. Your clients will feel like they are getting bonus information for free, while in reality you are keeping your business in your clients' minds so that if they decide they want another tattoo or piercing, they will think of your studio first. And you've made it easy for them because you have included your contact information for them in your newsletter!

You should also consider adding an opt-out link at the bottom of your newsletters. People always like to have a choice of whether to continue receiving information by email. Making it difficult to opt out can frustrate people and discourage them from patronizing your business. Note that in some areas, an opt-out link is mandatory.

6. Attend Tattoo Conventions

Participating in tattoo conventions is a great way to attain more clients as well as network with others in the business. You can learn many great things at conventions such as what your competitors are doing that is unique, what the latest industry trends are, and most important, gain new and repeat customers.

Many people who attend these conventions want to get inked or pierced while they are there, so make sure you and your artists are prepared to put in long days. Also, make sure your artists get adequate breaks for meals and rest times. You don't want your artists looking burnt out when you are essentially trying to sell their work.

Tattoo conventions are a good way to market; however, you must remember to market to your area. If you go to a convention in Seattle, Washington, to market your business when you are located in Great Falls, Montana, you probably won't get many, if any, customers from the convention to go to your studio back home. But if your business is in, for example, southern Alberta, and you know a lot of people will travel from your area to Calgary, Alberta, for a convention, then you may want to consider having a booth at the Calgary convention to create more awareness within your local market. A two- to three-hour driving radius is about the extent of your local market, so keep that in mind when you are considering convention venues.

Your exhibit should entice clients, so location at the event can be extremely important. You will have to pay more for a good location, but it may be worth it from all the clients you connect with. A high-traffic area or a place near the main doors of the event can pull potential clients to your booth first, which means you need to impress them in order to get them to take a business card, or better yet, get a tattoo or piercing at the event.

In order to entice people you need to make sure your artists and piercers are welcoming. Having your staff there to explain and show off their best work in their portfolios will help gain attendees' attention. Also, having good lighting on artists that are currently working on clients will show the art as it is being created.

Make sure the signage on your booth is well lit and easily readable so that attendees remember your booth. They may return later for a piercing, or they may remember your business in the future when they are looking for a studio that provides great tattoos.

Make sure you have lots of business cards to hand out to potential clients. Also, you may want to sell merchandise such as T-shirts, bags, or other promotional products that include your business name and logo.

Holding a daily draw at your booth with prizes that include small tattoos, piercings, gift cards, or merchandise can generate a buzz.

Another way to garner future clients is to sell gift cards at your booth. Gift cards promote your business as well as bring in new clients, because they are usually gifted to others that will either be new to your studio, or regulars that frequent your business.

You could include a selection of body jewelry for attendees to buy. If you do sell jewelry, you should put the merchandise in a glass case to prevent any products from going "missing" or being handled by people not interested in buying. You should have your body piercer there to help answer any questions customers may have about jewelry and piercings in general.

7. Promotional Merchandise

Once you are up and running and can afford to invest in promotional merchandise, you may want to consider doing so. Selling T-shirts, hats, bumper stickers, bags, flasks, or other promotional products that include branding such as your business name and logo may increase consumers' awareness of your business.

Company-branded merchandise is a great way to spread the word about your business, but the important thing is to remember to make sure it is not just a plain advertisement on a product. It has to have a "cool factor" in order for people to want to purchase it. Having a great logo or great art on the merchandise will be the key to selling it.

8. Recognition of Your Artists' Work

An interesting way to advertise is to encourage your artists to get recognition for themselves in the tattoo community. Getting your studio artists to enter their best or most interesting work in tattoo competitions and magazines will help boost their names and your studio's reputation. The more known the artist is, the more clients will come to your studio.

Having artists display awards or certificates at their workstations or up front in the studio will help gain new clients and repeat customers to your studio. Also, you can tie this type of advertising in with contacting the local news to see if they will run a story on your artists' achievements.

9
Hiring Tattoo Artists

Searching for the right employees for your studio will be time consuming, but worth it if you take the time to find artists that will fit your brand and your team. You want everyone to be able to get along, with no diva or rock star behavior. You also want to make sure your studio's reputation is represented well by the people you hire.

1. Hiring and Interviewing Tattoo Artists

Finding great artists and retaining them will be one of the most difficult and never ending problems you will face when you are hiring artists.

Choose your tattoo artists carefully as their work will influence the public and thus your

business. Do not be afraid to trust your instinct and never hire a tattoo artist you would not let tattoo you and your family. Remember that tattoos are considered a minor surgical procedure and should never be taken lightly as people's health can be at risk if procedures are not followed properly. Also, tattoos are for life so a bad tattoo can affect your studio for years to come. Be very selective in choosing artists. A great tattoo artist can do more for your studio than any amount of advertising, as his or her work is out in the public every day with people asking, "Where did you get that tattoo?" Clients may remember the artist who did their tattoo but they will almost always remember the studio's name.

1.1 Where to find great artists

The Internet is a great tool for finding artists. There are numerous websites dedicated to tattoo artists looking for work and tattoo studios looking to hire. A major hurdle to cross if you are not a tattoo artist is attracting tattoo artists with talent so you will have to be inventive such as offering a signing bonus, paying for their relocation and accommodations, or offering a good percentage of commission. If you do not have something to offer the tattoo artist, you will find it near impossible to attract good artistic talent and you will have to settle for average to subpar or apprentice artists.

Tattoo artists who are good will have a clientele following so when you secure an artist you will also gain his or her clients (theoretically if the tattoo artist was already working in the same city you are opening in). New artists or subpar artists will have no clientele base, and their reputations will hinge greatly on your studio.

If the location you are opening in is a larger city or a tourist area, you will have a greater selection of tattoo artists to choose from and will have a better chance of retaining them. Keep in mind that artists, in general, tend to be transient in nature. It is well known that tattoo artists like to travel and move around so getting your studio on a guest artist circuit can keep tattoo artists applying at your studio as they move about.

In order to get on the guest artist circuit, you will need to be in business for awhile. You will also need to have lots of industry recognition such as published articles about your studio and artists. If your business is well known, good artists will come to you asking if you are accepting guest artists. At conventions, artists will look at your portfolios and decide whether your business is somewhere they would like to work in a temporary guest position.

In larger centers there can be coverage by media such as magazines and television that feature truly skilled artists. This can be a great draw for future artists if you can gain media coverage. A common trait in all great tattoo artists is a love for art, in any form.

In your advertisement for artists you may want to include the following:

- How many years' experience the artist has to have (e.g., five years' experience).
- Whether they will need to have their own equipment, inks, and medical supplies such as gloves.
- How long the artist will be on probation.
- Hours and days of operation that the artist will be expected to work.

1.2 Interviewing artists

Any artist you are serious about hiring should have experience in drawing, sculpture, painting, photography, computer design, or some other form of artistic expression. This ensures that your tattoo artist will not be a "human photocopier" and will know the basics, such as what colors work together in shading, best body placements for tattoos, and if the person is able to make changes to tattoo designs as necessary. The majority of tattoo work sought out by clients is custom artwork, meaning it has to be designed by the tattoo artist in order to meet the creative requirements of the client. Tattoo artists who have experience with computer-assisted design programs can be a great asset to your business as programs speed up design time so more tattoos can be done in a day, thus increasing revenue.

Tattoo artists who cannot draw will have a very difficult time gaining clients in today's market and will have to settle for using flash (i.e., images on a sheet of paper), which are in hundreds of tattoo studios around the world and are basically all the same designs. The flash form of tattoo art, commonly referred to as "pick and stick," is declining in demand and the focus is now on custom pieces that have to be drawn.

Another thing to pay attention to is that all tattoo artists have a different style and forte, such as portraits, color work, black and grey work, cover-up work, and wildlife. In other words, pick artists that fit within your studio's genre and brand, and hire artists with various skills to cover all your client needs.

With any potential new staff member, you want to make sure this individual will represent your studio with the utmost professionalism, be loyal, get along with the other staff members, treat you and the studio's clients with respect, and do amazing tattoos in a professional manner. That being said, as the owner, especially if you are one that is not an artist, never forget that your tattoo artist is the one with the skill level to bring in the clientele. You may own the studio, but if you don't respect your staff for what they contribute, it will begin to show in the quality of their artwork and the way they operate at your studio.

There are many books, online references in regards to the interviewing process, as well as concise and practical books from Self-Counsel Press such as *Employee Management for Small Business*. Always go with your gut instinct and avoid the temptation to second guess yourself or hire out of desperation. Hiring a tattoo artist because you need one and nobody has applied, or the artist was the best of the worst that applied, is never the best course of action. It could result in the artist you hired creating poor tattoos, or having no regard for the latest sterilization procedure causing an infection to a client, or defying state or provincial regulations and tattooing a minor, all of which could result in your studio being shut down, and legal and/or criminal charges being laid against your studio and the artist. You will learn along the way which personalities you can work with and which ones you cannot as you run your studio.

When you are interviewing, ask that the artist bring a portfolio of recent tattoo work from the last couple of years so you can see his or her current style and techniques. Ask to see any artwork he or she has created such as paintings, drawings, or airbrushings to see what other creative talents the artist possesses. This will show the person's level of talent and potential for creating original designs. Look at the artist's portfolio as this will indicate the level and quality of work the artist is producing as well as his or her forte or style. As pictures in a portfolio can be falsified it is a good idea to give the artist a week-long trial at your studio to see exactly what level of skill the artist is at in a professional setting. This will give you an indication of artistic range.

Some studios require a potential employee to do an "interview piece," which is having the artist come to the interview with his or her own equipment and a client. The interviewee will do a demonstration of his or her work in front of the management. This provides you with an idea of how the person works with equipment, cleaning, and aftercare instructions to the client.

Also the longer the tattoo artist has been tattooing the more specific the person will be in his or her requirements of your studio, so be prepared to be flexible. With any new artist (especially subcontractors) it is recommended that you have a legal contract signed between you, defining what hours you expect worked, time off, what his or her job at your studio entails, the rate of pay, and duration of employment.

You may also want to specify whether you want the artist to take on apprentices while the person is employed in your studio. Not every artist will do this, and the person may not be suitable for mentorship. So keep that in mind when you are interviewing potential artists. You don't want to force someone to train when that is not something he or she enjoys or is good at. At the same time, you don't want to lose a potentially great employee just because he or she won't train apprentices.

1.3 References and background checks

If you plan to hire an already established tattoo artist, then you will want to talk to the previous studios the person was employed at. Always remember that in this industry other studios will, nine times out of ten, not be helpful, and could give you false information so take what they say with a grain of salt, and follow your own gut instinct.

You will also want to make sure an artist has all his or her licenses and necessary certification in the prevention of spreading bloodborne pathogens for your area. Many jurisdictions require artists to have their hepatitis vaccinations up-to-date before they can start work in a studio.

Also try to find clients that the tattoo artist has worked on before and get their opinions. Ask for client references and then call them.

2. Training Tattoo Apprentices

Training tattoo apprentices is a completely unregulated aspect of the tattoo and piercing industry. There are no accredited schools or colleges that offer instruction or give a state- or provincial-wide or Federal government accepted certification for the skill of tattooing or piercing.

The only way to become a tattoo artist is to find a tattoo artist in the industry who is willing to impart his or her knowledge, and get an apprenticeship from him or her. This can be extremely difficult as there is no standard price for an apprenticeship, no standard length of time, no standard on skills and/or topics taught to the apprentice, and virtually no guarantee on the quality of instruction.

Not all tattoo artists will train apprentices and those who will are usually very selective. It is not recommended that a tattoo artist take on an apprentice until he or she has a minimum of ten years of tattoo experience.

Since there is no regulation regarding apprenticeships in the industry, often, those who are considered novice artists at best are the ones handing out the instructions at an alarming rate. The usual length of time for a tattoo apprenticeship is one to four years. This time line can also vary greatly, depending on the apprentice; how fast the person progresses and how much time he or she can dedicate to learning the art. Anything less than a year is not enough instructional and training time to truly offer a well-rounded apprenticeship, and anything more than four years would be excessive, and equally unrealistic.

If you are the tattoo artist training an apprentice this can be a great source of revenue as apprenticeships can run anywhere from $4,000 to $15,000. Not to mention the added bonus of free labor, as most apprenticeships require the apprentice to be working around the studio learning and contributing to all aspects of tattooing while training. Usually, the studio takes a percentage of this fee toward any medical equipment the apprentice will use during his or her training, and to cover costs of lost revenue once the apprentice earns his or her time to work on skin. Again, as there is no regulation as to fees for an apprenticeship or the percentage owned to a studio for taking on an apprentice. It will vary from artist to artist, studio to studio.

Just remember that every apprentice you train has the potential to become a competing artist and could one day open a studio in close proximity to yours. It is highly recommended to have a legal contract between you and the apprentice to protect yourself, your studio, and to assist with the prevention of trade secrets being shared or used outside of the apprenticeship. This contract should clearly explain what the apprentice will be taught, what equipment if any is included, what is expected of the apprentice, the length of time, and the cost of the apprenticeship, and when payments are due.

3. Artist and Apprentice Contracts

Taking on apprentices for piercing and tattooing as well as trained artists means you will have to create employment agreements. This is important to ensure you protect your reputation and business secrets. The following sections cover what should go into your employment contracts. On the CD you will find templates that you can adjust to work for your business.

Note that you should have a lawyer look over any contract you create to make sure the contract is legal and binding.

3.1 Covenants of the studio

The covenants of the studio is the area in which you outline what you will provide to the artists, meaning the area in which the artist will work, whether the person will have his or her own room or workstation, the hours and days the space will be available to the person, what equipment will be supplied, and any other rules and regulations you expect employees to follow while working in your studio.

3.2 Covenants of the artist

The covenants of the artist covers the non-compete and nondisclosure area of the contract. You want to make sure that if the artist leaves, he or she will not be taking your business contacts with him or her. You don't want the person to take any trade secrets you have, your list of clients and their buying habits, financial information, business plans, or anything else you don't want in your competitors' hands.

You also don't want an artist to come in and learn your business, only for the person to quit and open a studio across the street from your studio. For example, you want to make sure in your contract that it says that the person cannot compete with your business within 30 miles of your studio. That way it prevents the person from being a direct competitor, for example, by setting up shop in your neighborhood.

You need to also clarify how long after the person quits (e.g., for three years) that this location stipulation is in place. Note that it has to be reasonable, and you cannot expect the law to uphold a contract that says the person must stay out of your area for a lifetime. (See Sample 6.)

You also don't want the artist to convince your other employees to go with him or her to another place of business. Again, this is because your former workers would be in direct competition with your business and take their clients with them.

3.3 Covenants of the trainer

In a trainer and apprentice agreement, the covenants of the trainer outline what exactly the trainer will provide for the apprentice. For a tattoo artist training an apprentice, the covenants may cover the tattoo techniques, machine maintenance, setup and building of the equipment, sterilization and disinfecting tools and techniques, as well as bedside manner and training.

3.4 Covenants of the apprentice

The covenants of the apprentice are similar to the covenants of the artist discussed in section **3.2**. You want to make sure that once the apprentice is trained that he or she will not take off and start his or her own business, which will compete with your business.

It is important that the person understands that by signing the agreement that he or she will not be able to take any trade secrets, client lists and their buying habits, the studio's financial information, business plans, or trade secrets with him or her.

You should also make sure to add a line about the apprentice not being able to compete within a minimum of 30 miles of your business if he or she does quit. You will have to outline how long the location stipulation is in place.

Note that in an apprenticeship agreement you will need to specify how much it will cost the apprentice to learn the trade. (See Sample 7.)

3.5 General provisions

The general provisions in the agreement describe any additional rules to be followed by both parties such as that both parties agree and understand the agreement. Also, that if there are any modifications to the agreement, the change must be agreed upon and it must be initialed or signed beside by both parties.

It also outlines what jurisdiction and laws the contract and parties are bound by.

3.6 Signing the contract

When the parties have agreed to everything in the contract, both parties must sign the contract and have it witnessed.

A good idea is to also have both parties and the witness initial each page of the contract. This prevents someone from replacing a page in the contract at a later time without the other party knowing of the switch.

Sample 6 can be altered to work for a piercer. A template can be found on the CD that can be used for hiring a body piercer.

4. How to Pay Your Artists

For the most part, tattoo artists are independent contractors. This means that they are responsible for their own taxes and insurance. There are two ways you can contract your artists — either by booth rental or percentage of sales.

The advantage to the percentage system is that the busier an artist is, the more money for the owner. The disadvantage is that this amount can fluctuate, which means you will have trouble estimating studio income each month unless your artists are booked months in advance. Also, if you are in a tourist destination, your studio may only be busy for a few months a year, meaning your artists won't be bringing in much during the off season.

When offering a percentage, the average is 60 percent of each sale goes to the artist if he or she uses his or her own supplies. If the studio owner offers the supplies, then the artist gets 50 percent of the sale. If the artist has recently finished an apprenticeship, he or she may take home only 40 or 50 percent for the first while. Raises in percentage may happen

Sample 6
Tattoo Artist Employment Agreement

For reference, this Agreement is dated: August 1, 20--

Between:

<u>   John Doe, Studio Owner   </u>
Who resides at_____
(hereinafter referred to as "Owner")

-and-

<u>   Janet Ice, Tattoo Artist   </u>
Who resides at_____
(hereinafter referred to as "Artist")

1.   Background

The Artist wishes to be employed in the trade of tattooing with Studio X (hereinafter referred to as "Studio").

In consideration of the mutual promises contained in this Agreement, as well as other good and valuable consideration, the receipt of which is hereby acknowledged, the Owner and the Artist (collectively referred to as the "Parties") agree as follows:

2.   Covenants of the Studio

The Studio will provide the Artist with the following:

    a.   A room or station to perform the procedures;

    b.   The room or station will be available to the Artist Monday through Thursday, from 12 p.m. to 8 p.m. *(specify days and hours)*;

    c.   The Artist will work Monday through Thursday, from 12 p.m. to 8 p.m. *(specify hours and/or days)*;

    d.   Drawings for clients are expected in a timely manner;

    e.   Professional behavior is expected at all times;

    f.   The Studio will supply _____ *(specify equipment, medical supplies, etc., that are supplied by Owner)* and office supplies;

    g.   The Studio will supply advertising and coupons;

    h.   The rooms or stations will be in good repair; and

    i.   The Studio complies with all health and safety guidelines set out by the local health authority.

3.   Covenants of the Artist

The Artist acknowledges that during the course of employment he/she will acquire information about certain matters that are confidential to the Studio, which information is the exclusive property of the studio, including but not limited to, the following:

SELF-COUNSEL PRESS — START & RUN A TATTOO & BODY PIERCING STUDIO/11

a.   Trade secrets;

b.   Lists of present and prospective customers and buying habits;

c.   Purchase requirements;

d.   Pricing and sales policies and concepts;

e.   Financial information;

f.   Business plans, forecasts, and marketing strategies; and

g.   Discoveries, inventions, research and development, formulas, and technology.

3.1   The Artist acknowledges that the information could be used to the detriment of the Studio and that the disclosure could cause irreparable harm to the Studio. Accordingly, the Artist undertakes to treat confidentially all information and not to disclose it to any third party or to use it for any purpose either during employment, except as it may be necessary in the proper discharge of ~~his/~~her duties, or after termination of employment for any reason, except with the written permission of the Studio.

3.2   The Artist agrees with and for the benefit of the Studio that for a period of <u>three (3) years</u> from the date of the termination of employment, the Artist will not directly or indirectly:

a.   Carry on, be engaged in, concerned with, interested in, or permit ~~his/~~her name or any part thereof to be used or employed in a business which is the same as, or competitive with, the business of the Owner, including, but not limited to, any business related to tattooing, within the geographical area of the City of _____, in the State/~~Province~~ of_____, and a radius of <u>thirty (30)</u> miles/~~kilometers~~ from the City of_____, in the State/~~Province~~ of_____; except where the Artist is employed by the Owner of __Studio X__ *(insert name of business)*.

b.   Attempt to induce any person who, as of the date hereof or at any time during the term of employment for the Studio, to engage in any of the activities hereby described under clause 3.2a above, or attempt to induce any such person to terminate his or her employment with the Studio.

c.   Attempt to direct or take away business or clients from the Studio.

4.   General Provisions

a.   This Agreement contains the final and entire understanding and agreement between the Parties with respect to the terms and conditions of the employment stressed within.

b.   Any modification of this Agreement must be in writing and signed by both Parties or it shall have no effect and shall be null and void.

c.   This Agreement shall ensure to the benefit of and be binding upon the Parties hereto together with their respective heirs, executors, administrators, successors, and assigns.

d.   The Parties acknowledge that they have read and understood this Agreement and are under no distress about it.

e.   For the purpose of the entire Agreement, time is of the essence.

SELF-COUNSEL PRESS — START & RUN A TATTOO & BODY PIERCING STUDIO/11

f.   This Agreement shall be governed by and constructed in accordance with the laws by the State/Province of_____.

The Parties have signed this Agreement and had it witnessed on _____,
(day, month, year)

at the City of _____, in the State/Province of _____.

_____John Doe_____
John Doe

_____Janet Ice_____
Janet Ice

Signed by _____John Doe_____
in the presence of:

Signed by _____Janet Ice_____
in the presence of:

_____
(Signature of witness)

_____
(Print name of witness)

_____
(Address of witness)

_____
(Occupation of witness)

_____
(Signature of witness)

_____
(Print name of witness)

_____
(Address of witness)

_____
(Occupation of witness)

Sample 7
Tattoo Artist Apprenticeship Agreement

For reference, this Agreement is dated: _August 1, 20--_

Between:

<u>Jim Smith, a Tattoo Artist</u>

Who resides at_____

(hereinafter referred to as "Trainer")

-and-

<u>Trudy Boxer, Media/Graphics Specialist</u>

Who resides at_____

(hereinafter referred to as "Apprentice")

1.   Background

The Apprentice wishes to receive training in the trade of tattooing with the Trainer, a tattoo artist at <u>Studio X</u> (hereinafter referred to as "Studio"), is able and willing to train the Apprentice in the trade of Tattooing.

In consideration of the mutual promises contained in this agreement, the full sum of $_____ will be received up front. As well as other good and valuable consideration, the receipt of which is hereby acknowledged, the Apprentice and Trainer (hereinafter known as the "Parties") agree as follows:

2.   Covenants of the Trainer

The Trainer will provide the Apprentice with on the job training including but not limited to tattooing techniques, machine maintenance, setup and building, machine parts, grips, tubes and stems, sterilization and disinfecting of the tools, bedside manner, history, and the training manual. Understanding of basic human biology and anatomy and instructions on disinfecting and cleansing of the human body will be provided, as well as cross contamination information and procedures related to this. This fee will also include all equipment or some equipment which includes _____ *(machine, parts, power box, clip cords, ink and needles, etc.).*

3.   Covenants of the Apprentice

3.1   The Apprentice acknowledges that during the course of the apprenticeship he/she will acquire information about certain matters that are confidential to the Trainer, which information is the exclusive property of the Trainer, including but not limited to, the following:

   a.   Trade secrets;

   b.   Lists of present and prospective customers and buying habits;

   c.   Purchase requirements;

   d.   Pricing and sales policies and concepts;

   e.   Financial information;

   f.   Business plans, forecasts, and marketing strategies; and

   g.   Discoveries, inventions, research and development, formulas, and technology.

SELF-COUNSEL PRESS — START & RUN A TATTOO & BODY PIERCING STUDIO/11

3.2 The Apprentice acknowledges that the information could be used to the detriment of the Trainer and that the disclosure could cause irreparable harm to the Trainer. Accordingly, the Apprentice undertakes to treat confidentially all the information and not to disclose it to any third party or to use it for any purpose either during the apprenticeship, except as it may be necessary in the proper discharge of his/her duties, or after termination of the apprenticeship for any reason, except with the written permission of the Trainer.

3.3 The Apprentice agrees with and for the benefit of the Trainer that for a period of <u>three (3) years</u> from the date of the termination of apprenticeship, the Apprentice will not directly or indirectly:

    a. Carry on, be engaged in, concerned with, interested in, or permit his/her name or any part thereof to be used or employed in a business which is the same as, or competitive with, the business of the Trainer, including, but not limited to, any business related to tattooing, within the geographical area of the City of_____, in the State/Province of _____, and within a radius of <u>thirty (30)</u> miles/kilometers from the City of_____, in the State/Province of_____, except where the Apprentice is employed by the Trainer of <u>Studio X</u>.

    b. Attempt to induce any person who, as of the date hereof or at any time during the term of the apprenticeship or employment for the Trainer, to engage in any of the activities hereby described under clause 3.3a above, or attempt to induce any such person to terminate his or her employment with the Trainer.

    c. Attempt to direct or take away business or customers from the Trainer.

4. General Provisions

    a. This Agreement contains the final and entire understanding and agreement between the parties with respect to the terms and conditions of the apprenticeship stressed within.

    b. Any modification of this Agreement must be in writing and signed by both the Trainer and the Apprentice or it shall have no effect and shall be null and void.

    c. This Agreement shall ensure to the benefit of and be binding upon the parties hereto together with their respective heirs, executors, administrators, successors, and assigns.

    d. The parties acknowledge that they have read and understood this Agreement and are under no distress about it.

    e. For the purpose of the entire Agreement time is of the essence.

Sample 7 — Continued

f.   This Agreement shall be governed by and constructed in accordance with the laws by the
~~State~~/Province of_____.

The Parties have signed this Agreement and had it witnessed on _____,
                                                                            (day, month, year)
at the City of _____, in the State/Province of _____.

_____   _____
          Jim Smith   Trudy Boxer
          Jim Smith   Trudy Boxer

Signed by _____Jim Smith_____   Signed by _____Trudy Boxer_____
in the presence of: in the presence of:

_____   _____
     (Signature of witness)   (Signature of witness)

_____   _____
     (Print name of witness)   (Print name of witness)

_____   _____
     (Address of witness)   (Address of witness)

_____   _____
     (Occupation of witness)   (Occupation of witness)

with increased experience and repeat clients, or by bringing in more clients.

If you choose to go with the booth rental, then you will always have a steady income even during slow times. However, the steady income means no increase in funds during busy times. If you go with the booth rental system, you will need to set a date each month when the rent is due.

You can choose to pay employees daily or weekly with cash or write checks for credit card sales. It is important that you keep records of payments for tax purposes.

Note that location of the studio also contributes to how much an artist makes. In a rural area, where business is less than in a busy metropolis or tourist area, the person will get paid less because they may have to charge less than big-city prices.

Benefits are not usually offered by the owner. However, some studios offer benefits by increasing the percentage paid to the artist to make up for the artist having to pay his or her own health insurance costs. In most cases, since the work is usually subcontracted, there are no paid vacations, sick time, or overtime. If you want to entice good artists to your studio, or keep staff longer, you may want to offer benefits and bonuses. The better an artist is treated, the more likely the person is to stick around for a long time.

5. When an Artist Leaves

Artists leaving is an inevitability of hiring and working with tattoo artists. The reasons for losing artists will always vary. Life changes, people change, and then they move on. Even if you never have to fire an artist, some will leave your studio for any number of reasons so you must be prepared to deal with issues that can arise from this.

If a tattoo artist's client has prepaid for a tattoo and the tattoo is not finished, do you as the studio owner cover the cost of the tattoo and pay another one of your artists to finish the work? Or do you tell the client if he or she wants the tattoo finished at your studio, he or she will have to pay again? You could pay the tattoo artist for each session he or she does rather than paying the artist his or her whole percentage up front to avoid being out of pocket in a case like this.

Another issue that can occur is some clients will not be comfortable with another artist at your studio finishing the tattoo so you may lose the client; there is no way to avoid this other than offering the client a discount to try another artist at your studio.

If your artist gives you lots of notice that he or she is leaving, the artist may allow appointments for touch-ups and finishing tattoos previously started on clients during the last few months at your studio.

Also, some tattoos need touch-ups which are small fixes to tattoos, such as a line may be missing, or some color may have come out in the healing process so a tattoo artist will fix it. Some studios charge a fee for touch-ups, usually around $25 to $50 while other studios and/or their artists may not charge for this. There are positives and negatives to both. On the one hand, if touch-ups cost the client then if the tattoo artist leaves your studio you will not have to pay out of your pocket for another artist to do the touch-up, but the clients may see this as a double charge and that you do not stand behind your work. On the other hand, if there is no charge for touch-ups, the clients may not take good care of the tattoo in the healing process and if the artist leaves, you will have to pay another artist at your studio to do a touch-up.

Another problem that can arise is where clients have dropped off artwork to be altered for the tattoo, or where the artist has a drawing for the client, and the artist leaves. Check with your artist before he or she leaves to get any artwork that belongs to clients back and to check the status of existing drawings for clients.

10

Hiring Body Piercers

Many tattoo studios do not offer piercings; however, piercing is a complementary service that fits well with a tattoo studio and can bring in more clientele. If you want to have piercings as part of your studio, this chapter will help you with the hiring process.

1. Hiring and Interviewing Body Piercers

Piercers are a little easier to find than tattoo artists, in that an apprenticeship for piercing can be completed in a shorter period of time than that of a tattoo apprentice; ergo, a larger percentage of trained piercers are entering into the body modification industry sooner.

Choose your piercer carefully as his or her work will influence the public and thus your business. Do not be afraid to trust your instincts and never hire a piercer you would not let pierce you or your family. Remember that piercings are considered a minor surgical procedure and should never be taken lightly as your clients' well-being could be at risk if all procedures are not followed properly. You want your piercer to represent your studio and brand, so make sure you hire the right person to fit in with your other employees and clients.

1.1 How to find great piercers

Finding a skilled piercer with good people skills and good work ethic can be as challenging as hiring in any other profession. Not only should you only consider hiring piercers with a high skill level, their professionalism should stand out as well.

Skilled piercers possess considerable hand-eye coordination. A unique, yet useful technique to see if an individual is or will make a good piercer is to watch him or her play pool. It gives a great indication of his or her level of hand-eye coordination. This is not to say though, by any means, that all piercers are pool sharks!

Websites will be a great place to look and advertise for body piercers that need work. Also word of mouth in the industry may lead you to piercers that would be a perfect fit for your studio.

In your advertisement for piercers you may want to include the following:

🌹 How many years' experience the piercer has to have (e.g., two years' experience).

🌹 Whether he or she will need to have his or her own equipment, jewelry, and medical supplies such as gloves.

🌹 How long the person will be on probation.

🌹 Hours and days of operation that the piercer will be expected to work.

1.2 Interviewing piercers

You will want a piercer with an eye for detail, who is familiar with the concept of proper placement of jewelry on the body, along with what style and size of jewelry to use. Body jewelry is like clothing; it is size specific.

Look at the piercer's portfolio to see the range of piercings he or she can perform. Especially look at ear cartilage projects, as well as surface piercings and dermal anchors, as these require a higher level of skill than eyebrow and nostril piercings, for example.

Make sure that the angle of the piercings is good as well as the line of the piercings in regards to the surrounding body parts; for example, an eyebrow piercing should complement the angle to the chin and to the side of the face as well as the hairline, a skilled piercer will know how to do this and an unskilled piercer will not.

As with tattoo artists, keep in mind that if you are an owner who is not part of the artistic workforce, your piercer's skill is his or her contribution to your business and its level of success. Always maintain communication with, and appreciation of, your piercer to promote respect of your ownership. A happy piercer can help to ensure a successful studio.

You want to make sure the piercer will represent your studio with the utmost professionalism, be loyal, and get along with other staff members. If you find someone that you think will fit in with other employees, bring the person in and have a group interview, encouraging fellow staff members to ask the person questions to see how well they will get along with the new person.

A good practice is to try the piercer out for a week at your studio, only permitting select piercings so you can see how they are placed and how they heal, and by asking the clients to come back in a week to see the piercings.

You may also want the potential employee to do a body piercing interview piece in which he or she brings in a client and demonstrates his or her ability to pierce. This will show you what the person's bedside manner is like and how he or she describes aftercare and so forth.

A well-trained piercer should have extensive, practical knowledge outside of the actual piercing procedures; he or she should know what happens with pregnant women who have navel piercings, and also know about nipple piercings and breastfeeding. The piercer must also know the importance of jewelry placement with oral piercings so as not to cause tooth and gum damage and/or erosion, and when downsizing oral piercings is a must.

Knowledge of aftercare of the piercing once the client leaves the studio is mandatory. A true professional will always send clients off with a sheet of all aftercare instructions, and an aftercare product to clean with, or information about what aftercare product to purchase and where.

You may also want your piercer to train apprentices. This may be a turn off for some experienced piercers because they either do not like training or they are not skilled as trainers. (Note that just because the person isn't a good trainer, does not mean he or she is a bad piercer. Training is a skill set not everyone has the patience or ability to do.) It doesn't hurt to ask before you give the person the job whether he or she would be willing to train others. If the answer is no, but you still want this person to work for you, then respect his or her decision and put apprenticeship training on hold until you hire someone who is willing to take on an apprentice.

If you are hiring a piercer who has been in the industry for years, the person may be slightly more demanding than newer piercers regarding what he or she wants when it comes to working for your studio. If the person is well known, it may be worth it for you to accommodate the person's demands (within reason, of course).

1.3 References and background checks for piercers

Similar to checking a tattoo artist's background and references, you will want to talk to previous studios where the person was employed.

Note that this is a competitive industry, and other studios may not be helpful, so you may have to go with your gut feeling.

You will also want to make sure the piercer has all the licenses and necessary certification for the prevention of spreading bloodborne pathogens. Many jurisdictions require piercers to have their hepatitis vaccinations up-to-date before they can start work in a studio.

Try to find clients the piercer has pierced before and get their opinions on the experience.

2. Training Piercing Apprentices

The same as with tattooing, piercing apprenticeships are a completely unregulated aspect of the tattoo and piercing industry. There are no accredited schools or colleges that offer instruction or give state- or province-wide or federal government accepted certification for the skill of piercing.

There are some self-proclaimed "piercing schools" that offer piercing instruction and a few people have been trained by them; however, when these "trained" piercers seek employment in the industry they find it difficult, because not enough practical experience was gained, or they might have to be retrained because not all topics were covered in the training.

The best way for a potential piercer to learn is to find a skilled and experienced piercer, and apply for an apprenticeship under that person. Keep in mind "skilled" and "experienced" are very different things. Again, do your research; just because an individual has been performing piercing procedures for a certain length of time does not necessarily mean he or she is skilled enough or comfortable with training others. Remember, you want apprentices and experienced piercers who will always represent your studio with their best work.

The apprenticeship fee can vary from studio to studio, as there is no standard price for an apprenticeship, no standard length of time, no standard on skills and/or topics taught to the apprentice, and no guarantee on the quality of instruction.

Again, as with tattoo artists, not all piercers will train apprentices and those who will are usually very selective. It is not recommended a piercer take on an apprentice until the person has a minimum of five years of piercing experience.

Training of piercers is quicker and less involved than tattoo apprenticeships. Piercings are not permanent, there are no intricate mechanical aspects to piercing, and no traditional artistic skill is required. A typical piercing apprenticeship lasts anywhere from six months to one year as anything shorter is not enough time to properly learn all the skills required and anything longer is unnecessary.

A piercing apprenticeship requires training in anatomy, sterilization processes, bloodborne pathogens, body jewelry, and aftercare instructions for the piercings, as well as the actual piercing and stretching procedures. Also the apprenticeship should include at least one of every piercing performed on a client or friend that knows that this is an apprentice that will be piercing him or her under the supervision of the trainer. This is usually done at a lowered cost and is a great way to get an apprentice some "hands on" training. This also allows for the practical knowledge of the apprentice to be gauged and critiqued, and gives a good indication as to when the apprentice will be ready to start piercing professionally.

Great emphasis should be placed on the fact that all piercings are a minor invasive procedure and should be treated as such. There are two piercings that can actually be fatal to the client if the procedure is preformed improperly; these are the navel and the tongue.

If the navel is pierced too deep it can result in perforated stomach lining and cause mass internal infection, capable of shutting down organs. A tongue piercing can be fatal if a main blood vessel is perforated, causing profuse bleeding if it is not cauterized in time. Extreme caution and professionalism is required for all piercings, but navel and tongue piercings most of all should never be attempted by a novice.

3. Body Piercer and Apprentice Contracts

Taking on apprentices for piercing as well as hiring trained piercers means you will have to create employment agreements. This type of contract contains similar information to what was provided in Chapter 9 for tattoo artists. Contracts are important to ensure you protect your reputation and business secrets. The following sections cover what should go into your employment contracts along with a sample body piercer apprenticeship agreement. On the CD you will find templates that you can adjust to work for your studio's hiring needs.

3.1 Covenants of the studio

The covenants of the studio is the area in which you outline what you will provide for the piercer, meaning the area the piercer will work, whether the person will have his or her own room or station, the hours and days the space will be available to the person, what equipment will be supplied, and any other rules and regulations you expect employees to follow while working in your studio.

It is recommended you have a contract drawn up that covers prevention of trade secrets being shared or used outside of the studio by an apprentice or experienced piercer. If it is an apprentice contract, it should clearly explain what the apprentice will be taught, what equipment if any is included, what is expected of the apprentice, the length of time and the cost of the apprenticeship and when payments are due. To create an employee contract, review Sample 6 in Chapter 8. On the CD you will find a Body Piercer Employment Agreement template that you can tweak to suit your studio's needs.

3.2 Covenants of the piercer

The covenants of the piercer covers the noncompete and nondisclosure area of the contract. You want to make sure that if the piercer leaves your employ, he or she will not take your business contacts and secrets with him or her. You don't want the person to take any trade secrets you have, your list of clients and their buying habits, financial information, business plans, or anything else you don't want in your competitors' hands.

You also don't want a piercer to learn your business, and then leave and join a competitor's studio. For example, you want to make sure your contract says that the piercer cannot compete with your business within 30 miles of your studio for a certain number of years after he or she quits working for you. Note that the time limit has to be within reason because you cannot expect the law to uphold a contract that says the person must stay out of your area for the next 50 years!

You also don't want the piercer to convince your other employees to go with him or her to another place of business, or to open their own business. Again, this is because your former workers would be in direct competition with your business.

3.3 Covenants of the piercing trainer

In a trainer and apprentice agreement, the covenants of the trainer outlines what exactly the trainer will provide for the apprentice. Besides training in the art of piercing, the piercing trainer may provide an apprentice with piercing tools, sterilization and disinfecting tools and techniques, bedside manner tips, and so forth.

3.4 Covenants of the piercing apprentice

The covenants of the apprentice are similar to the covenants of the piercer discussed earlier in section **3.2**. You want to make sure that once the apprentice is trained that he or she will not take off and start his or her own business or work with a competitor, which will compete with your business.

It is important that the apprentice understands that by signing the agreement that he or she will not be able to take any trade secrets, client lists and their buying habits, the studio's financial information, business plans, or trade secrets with him or her.

You should also make sure to add a line about the apprentice not being able to compete within a minimum of 30 miles of your business if he or she does quit or get fired. Note that you will have to outline how long the location stipulation is in place.

In an apprenticeship agreement you will need to specify how much it will cost the apprentice to learn the trade. (See Sample 8.) If you are the piercer training an apprentice this can be a great source of revenue as apprenticeships can cost the apprentice anywhere from $1,000 to $5,000, not to mention the added bonus of free labor, as most apprenticeships require the apprentice to be working at the studio for free while training. Just remember that every apprentice you train has the potential to become a competing piercer, and could one day open a studio in close proximity to yours or work for your competition.

Just as with tattoo apprenticeships there is no regulation for piercing apprenticeships, so fees to the artist and to the studio will have to be discussed and agreed upon prior to the commencement of any training. A portion of the fees do go to the studio for supplies provided to the apprentice piercer.

3.5 General provisions

The general provisions in the agreement describe any additional rules to be followed by both parties such as that both parties agree and understand the agreement. Also, that if there are any modifications to the agreement, the change must be agreed upon and initialed or signed beside by both parties.

It also outlines what jurisdiction and laws the contract and parties are bound by.

3.6 Signing the contract

When the parties have agreed to everything in the contract, both parties must sign the contract and have it witnessed.

A good idea is to also have both parties and the witness initial each page of the contract. This prevents someone from replacing a page in the contract at a later time without the other party knowing of the switch.

4. How to Pay Your Piercers

Offering a good percentage on commission is a good start to finding a great piercer; the standard rate is usually around 40 to 50 percent of the piercing rate, but offering a slightly higher rate is an excellent incentive for a piercer to choose your studio. Also try signing bonuses,

and offer help with relocation costs such as accommodation and travel expenses, to entice the really good piercers to your studio.

With any new piercer to your studio (especially one being subcontracted) it is recommended that you have a legal contract signed between you and him or her, defining what hours you expect worked, time off, what his or her job at your studio entails, and the rate of pay, as well as the duration of employment.

For the most part, piercers are independent contractors. This means that they are responsible for their own taxes and insurance.

Benefits are not usually offered by the owner. However, some studios offer benefits by increasing the percentage paid to the piercer to make up for the piercer having to pay for his or her own health insurance costs. In most cases, since the work is usually subcontracted, there are no paid vacations, sick time, or overtime. If you want to entice good piercers to your studio, or keep staff longer, you may want to offer benefits and bonuses. The better a piercer is treated, the more likely the person will stick around longer.

5. Dermal Anchoring, Surface Piercings, Stretching, and Suspension Piercings

If you are going to hire someone trained in dermal anchoring, surface piercings, stretching, or suspension piercings, the same rules as outlined in the previous sections apply. It is important that you, as the studio owner, understand these procedures so you know what to look for when hiring this type of specialized body piercer. The following is a brief outline of the procedures.

Body Piercer Apprenticeship Agreement

For reference, this Agreement is dated:_____

Between:

_____ Jocelyn Heartbreaker, Body Piercer _____
Who resides at_____
(hereinafter referred to as "Trainer")

-and-

_____ Ed Johnson _____
Who resides at_____
(hereinafter referred to as "Apprentice")

1. **Background:**

   The Apprentice wishes to receive training in the trade of body piercing with the Trainer, at _Studio X_ (hereinafter referred to as "Studio"). The Trainer is willing and able to train the Apprentice in the trade of Body Piercing.

   In consideration of the mutual promises contained in this agreement, the full sum of $_____ will be received up front and the remainder of $_____ will be received on _____ *(date)*. As well as other good and valuable consideration, the receipt of which is hereby acknowledged, the Trainer and Apprentice (collectively referred to hereinafter as the "Parties") agree as follows:

2. **Covenants of the Trainer**

   The Trainer will provide the Apprentice on the job training included but not limited to the piercing techniques, jewelry, piercing tools, sterilization and disinfecting of the tools, bedside manner, history, and training manual.

3. **Covenants of the Apprentice**

   3.1 The Apprentice acknowledges that during the course of the apprenticeship he/she will acquire information about certain matters that are confidential, which information is the exclusive property of the trainer, including but not limited to, the following:

   a. Trade secrets;

   b. Lists of present and prospective customers and buying habits;

   c. Purchase requirements;

   d. Pricing and sales policies and concepts;

   e. Financial information;

   f. Business plans, forecasts, and marketing strategies; and

   g. Discoveries, inventions, research and development, formulas, and technology.

3.2 The Apprentice acknowledges that the information could be used to the detriment of the Trainer and that the disclosure could cause irreparable harm to the Trainer. Accordingly, the Apprentice undertakes to treat confidentially all the information and not to disclose it to any third party or to use it for any purpose either during the apprenticeship, except as it may be necessary in the proper discharge of his/her duties, or after termination of the apprenticeship for any reason, except with the written permission of the Trainer.

3.3 The Apprentice agrees with and for the benefit of the Trainer that for a period of __three (3)__ years from the date of the termination of the apprenticeship, the Apprentice will not directly or indirectly:

    a. Carry on, be engaged in, concerned with, interested in, or permit his/her name or any part thereof to be used or employed in a business which is the same as, or competitive with, the business of the employer, including, but not limited to, any business related to piercing, within the geographical area of the City_____, in the State/Province of _____, and a radius of __thirty (30)__ miles/kilometers from the City of_____, in the State/Province of _____, except where the Apprentice is employed by the Trainer of __Studio X__ *(insert name of business).*

    b. Attempt to induce any person who, as of the date hereof or at any time during the term of the apprenticeship or employment for the Trainer, to engage in any of the activities hereby described under clause 3.3a above, or attempt to induce any such person to terminate his or her employment with the Trainer.

    c. Attempt to direct or take away business or customers from the Trainer.

4. General Provisions

    a. This Agreement contains the final and entire understanding and agreement between the parties with respect to the terms and conditions of the apprenticeship addressed within.

    b. Any modification of this Agreement must be in writing and signed by both the Trainer and the Apprentice or it shall have no effect and shall be null and void.

    c. This Agreement shall ensure to the benefit of and be binding upon the Parties hereto together with their respective heirs, executors, administrators, successors, and assigns.

    d. The Parties acknowledge that they have read and understood this Agreement and are under no distress about it.

    e. For the purpose of the entire Agreement time is of the essence.

f.   This Agreement shall be governed by and constructed in accordance with the laws by the State/~~Province~~ of _____ .

The Parties have signed this Agreement and had it witnessed on _____ ,

(day, month, year)

at the City of _____ , in the State/~~Province~~ of _____ .

_____*Jocelyn Heartbreaker*_____   _____*Ed Johnson*_____
Jocelyn Heartbreaker   Ed Johnson

Signed by _____Jocelyn Heartbreaker_____   Signed by _____Ed Johnson_____
in the presence of: in the presence of:

_____   _____
(Signature of witness)   (Signature of witness)

_____   _____
(Print name of witness)   (Print name of witness)

_____   _____
(Address of witness)   (Address of witness)

_____   _____
(Occupation of witness)   (Occupation of witness)

5.1 Dermal anchoring

A relatively new procedure in the world of piercing is dermal anchoring, which is semi-permanent implantation. The premise of the anchor is to allow the bodies' connective tissues and muscles to grow through the jewelry locking it into place. There are two methods used to insert dermal anchors; one is using traditional piercing needles and making an "x"-like insertion point and the other is to use a biopsy punch, which cuts out a circle of skin allowing the dermal anchor to be inserted. It will depend on your piercer's training as to which method he or she will use.

Removing a dermal anchor usually requires a scalpel and will leave a small scar. The advantage to dermal anchor procedures is that the finished project has less of a rejection rate than the traditional method. This goes double for placements in high motion areas. The dermal anchor also allows for the look of a single bead instead of the traditional dual beads. (The CD includes pictures of dermal anchors as well as other types of piercings.)

A dermal anchor costs significantly more than traditional body jewelry, as do the replacement beads for the anchor, so you will have to charge more for this procedure. This can also mean higher profits depending on your market segment.

5.2 Surface piercings

Surface piercings are piercings that are by practical application intended to be temporary, as they are placed on areas of the body where there is no protrusion or fold of skin tissue. These can be simple piercings such as a navels all the way up to the more complicated corset piercings. Designs can be made on the skin using precise jewelry placement creating shapes such as stars, hearts, and geometric representations.

Surface piercings are typically put on parts of the body that will more than likely reject the piercing (push the piercing out of the body). This is due to the part of body selected being a high motion area, or the piercing going against the grain of the skin. The length of time the piercing holds before rejection varies on the piercing itself, the body part, the design selected, and the person's healing rate. Many other factors can contribute, but surface piercings will almost always reject at some point in time. The client must be aware of this fact and stop by the studio frequently to have the piercer check on the piercing and determine when to remove the jewelry.

If the rejection of the jewelry is caught at the onset, the significant scarring which can be caused by surface piercings can be avoided. Metal jewelry and polytetrafluoroethylene (PTFE) are used for surface piercings but PTFE is used significantly more than metal; however, it depends on the body part and the design of piercing as to which product is used. (The CD includes a couple of links to places that sell dermal and body piercing jewelry; pictures of the jewelry can be seen on their sites.) PTFE is a plastic product that uses Teflon to coat the porous material of the plastic. Porous materials, such as organic and some acrylic jewelry and uncoated plastic, can hold bacteria which can lead to infection during the initial piercing and healing time.

5.3 Stretching

With certain piercings; after the initial piercing is healed the client may wish to insert a larger size (gauge) of jewelry into the piercing; this is called stretching. A taper pin is used to accomplish this. The most common request for stretching is in the earlobes, with which clients can go up to large sizes of holes in the earlobes. This is achieved by stretching a few gauges at a time — usually no more than two — until the hole reaches the desired size. Once a client has gone up to or past a 0 gauge, the body generally will never be able to heal the hole. The hole will never close up again and plastic surgery will be required to fix it, if the client wishes to no longer wear the jewelry.

5.4 Suspension piercings

Suspension piercings are said to sometimes be used for meditation purposes, or to gain a higher level of spiritual awareness. They can be used as entertainment or as performance art as well. The process of piercing is very involved and difficult and should only be done by an experienced piercer to avoid serious injury. This process requires proper hook placement and an understanding of human anatomy and physiology. Multiple hooks are pierced around the shoulders, upper arm, and back, as well as around the knees to allow the individual to suspend from the ceiling or some sort of apparatus. If the number of hooks pierced are too few, the suspended individual's skin will be unable to withstand the body's weight and will rip.

11

Dealing with Employees

Tattoo artists can sometimes be transient in nature. They will stay on at a studio for a year or two and then move on to other locations in the same city, or a different city, state or province, or country. If your artist becomes world-renowned, he or she will more than likely move on to other places.

This chapter is about how to deal with employees. Keeping your employees happy leads to them staying longer and generates higher revenues by keeping their regular clients. You will need to offer incentives besides the benefits and bonuses mentioned in Chapters 9 and 10.

This chapter will also give you advice on how to deal with staff problems such as employee theft and how to fire employees.

1. Hiring a Front-Desk Employee

Your main employees will be tattoo artists and body piercers. However, you will also need to find help to cover the reception desk if you are not able to cover it, because you are one of the artists or you don't want to be in the studio every day. You may only need a part-time employee to cover your days off, while you're on vacation, if you are away sick, or because the studio is so busy.

Many studios require tattoo artists or piercers to answer the phone; however, this is a business decision that will be unique to each studio. Do you save money by having the tattoo artists or piercers answer the phone but potentially lose clients because the artists or piercers were working or not wanting to answer the phone? Keep in mind that once you hire an employee it is a commitment that comes with extra paperwork, vacation pay, holiday pay, and remittance of taxes to the government. Your front-desk employee is relying on you to pay him or her even if your studio has a bad week and makes little money.

Depending on the level of training and pay you want to give to your front-desk employee, you may want the person to be able to do the following:

- 🌹 Answer phones
- 🌹 Book appointments or give clients reminder calls
- 🌹 Take payments
- 🌹 Do bookkeeping
- 🌹 Sell jewelry or other merchandise
- 🌹 Client care
- 🌹 Cleaning
- 🌹 Inventory
- 🌹 Place medical, tattoo, and piercing supply orders

Your front staff member is more than likely the first person clients or potential clients will see when they come into your studio. They should be friendly and represent your brand. Hiring a person who is enthusiastic about the industry is key to making sure the first thing your clients see is a friendly and welcoming person. Many potential customers have walked out of studios and moved on to competitors due to condescending or ignorant staff members.

Some potential clients can be skittish when it comes to their first tattoo, so having someone there the greet them and be knowledgeable when answering their questions can go a long way to securing the clients' business.

Your front-desk employee cannot be on a contract, but instead must be hired as a salaried or hourly employee due to labor laws in North America. This rule applies to all businesses and is under the Federal Government's Common Law Rules of contract employees. If you have any uncertainty that the person you wish to hire is considered contracted staff or an employee you can file Form SS-8, "Determination of Worker Status for Purposes of Federal Employment Taxes and Income Tax Withholding" with the IRS. In Canada information on this can be obtained from Canada Revenue Agency.

This also means there are rules as to firing of or laying off of paid employees so be sure to research these regulations within your jurisdiction. When you are just starting out, you may not be able to pay much more than minimum wage to this employee. However, once your studio starts making a steady income, if your front-desk employee is really good at his or her job, you should try to make sure he or she has a reasonable wage. You want to keep good employees that will talk about you as a great boss. Word-of-mouth advertising is not just done by happy clients, but happy staff as well.

2. Aspire to Keep Your Staff Happy

Consider giving incentives to your staff. The longer you can keep tattoo artists and body piercers the better your business will be, because good staff means repeat clients and word-of-mouth advertising.

If your staff is doing a great job by showing up for work on time, bringing in a lot of new clients, and representing the business well, consider rewarding them. Incentives can be inexpensive or expensive depending on where your studio is financially. Many incentives can be tax writeoffs because they are considered business expenses. Check with your local tax authority to see if this is the case in your area.

Some of the incentives you may want to offer for a job well done include:

- Sports event or concert tickets
- A gift certificate for a round of golf
- Team-building activities such as closing the studio for the day (during non-busy times) and going out for a game of paintball or bowling
- Gift certificates to local restaurants, movie theaters, or bookstores
- A retreat for the whole staff to a beach resort or ski chalet
- Cakes or small presents on birthdays
- Bringing in a box of donuts and good coffee from Tim Hortons or Starbucks
- Parties or dinner celebrations for special holidays such as Christmas
- Deals on body jewelry, piercings, and tattoos
- Monetary bonuses
- Extra days off
- Letting the employee leave early or come in late on certain days

The key to giving a good gift is to make sure the recipient will enjoy it. If the person doesn't like golf, but enjoys reading, do not give a golf certificate but instead give him or her a gift certificate to use at the bookstore. Knowing your staff's likes and dislikes shows that you care and want to keep them happy.

You can do small things such as taking them out for lunch for staff meetings instead of holding the meetings in the studio. Being accommodating when staff need time off for family events or emergencies can also help keep staff satisfied with their job. Many artists enjoy this industry because it gives them the freedom to set work hours that are accommodating to their lifestyles.

Another thing that might not seem like an incentive, but is, can be offering the staff free coffee or having soda or juices available in the staff fridge. Just make sure no food or beverage products are in the tattoo and piercing rooms or workstations.

Another incentive is to have an open-door policy, meaning your staff can feel comfortable talking to you about ideas for business improvement or to air grievances. Trust with your staff is important in order to retain them and make them feel welcome. Showing your staff that you respect their opinions can go a long way to diverting problems as well as enhancing their work performance.

3. Dealing with Staff Problems

You will find that over the years of owning your studio that you will hire a few bad apples. Everyone hopes to avoid this, but it does happen. How you deal with a bad employee is important because you don't want to break labor laws in your area or end up with a lawsuit for unfair dismissal. Staff meetings are a great place to take preventive measures as problems can be highlighted in a positive environment, as well as provide a way to take documentation of the problem so that if it keeps happening you have written documentation to back up your decision.

3.1 Harassment

Labor codes usually specify that a business must have a harassment policy to protect employees and customers. As an owner, you are responsible for creating appropriate policies, implementing and monitoring the policies, and making sure all new and current employees understand them.

Harassment includes any improper behavior by a person that is directed at or offensive to another employee or client. The person has to have reasonably known that the offense was an objectionable act or comment that demeans, belittles, or causes personal humiliation or embarrassment to the other person. Any act of intimidation or threat is considered harassment.

Your first step in dealing with someone who is harassing other employees or clients is to take the person aside and talk to him or her. Review the harassment policy with the person. It may be that you need to mediate between the employees to come to a resolution. Keep a record of any harassment discussions for your files and to cover you in case you have to dismiss the harassing employee.

If the harassment continues, you will need to dismiss the employee so make sure you follow all of your local labor codes for the correct procedure.

If the person is threatening violence or stalking your employee, call the police immediately. The situation has escalated beyond your control.

The harassment information also applies to clients. You do not have to keep clients that are making your staff or you miserable. It's okay to fire a client.

3.2 Employee accountability

If you find that an employee is coming in late often, or not showing up for a shift at all without calling, then you need to consider the value of that employee. Is he or she worth keeping with all the disruptions in scheduling and appointments that he or she is causing? Do his or her clients understand and will they reschedule or are clients dropping like flies because of the flakiness of the artist or piercer?

If you find your artist or piercer is taking advantage of you, you may want to consider showing the person the rules of the studio or the contract the person signed, if you stipulated rules for no-shows or lateness or whatever the problem is.

You may want to punish the artist by suspending him or her for two or more shifts on a booth rental system, while the person still pays the full amount for the week. Or, if it happens often, you may want to reduce his or her take-home percentage. Another option is to offer the client that the artist was late or no showed on, a deal on the tattoo or piercing that comes out of the tattoo artist or piercer's percentage. If you decide to do either of these punishments, you should have them described in the hiring contracts. This may help you avoid running into any problems with local labor laws. Regardless, you should always check with your local jurisdiction to make sure you are following the rules.

3.3 Employee theft

Employee theft is a very difficult and time-consuming issue to actually prove. If it gets to court, it is always the decision of the court as to whether the person is guilty or not. You will want to make sure the amount stolen is worth the time, effort, and money that it will cost to press charges and go to court.

You will have to obtain a lawyer to represent you, file a theft report with the police, and pass on any evidence you may possess, and be available for all court dates. This can amount to a lot of time and money and, even if you win the case against your employee, artist, or piercer, you may not receive back the financial amount that was stolen. If you do win the case, the court may order that the amount be paid back in increments which can take years. The best way to prove theft is by videotaping your suspected employee as this will prove to the court and police that theft was occurring.

Another thing to consider in pressing or not pressing charges against the perpetrator is how other employees will handle the situation, as they might be called to court as witnesses to the crime. Consideration must be paid to the effect of a long drawn out court case on the morale of the studio.

3.4 Firing employees

If you have to fire an employee, review the employee contract before you go forth with the firing. You want to make sure you understand the terms in the agreement in order not to put yourself in a situation where you get sued for breach of contract.

It is best if you have given the employee verbal as well as written warnings to cover yourself and prevent your business being sued. It is important to document all the instances that have led up to the employee being fired. If you conduct employee evaluations, make sure you write out what the person needs to improve and get him or her to sign it. This way you have documented that the employee has understood the evaluation and what is expected of him or her to improve his or her work habits.

If the employee has access to business files or keys to the studio, you will need to get these back before you fire him or her. This way you are not having to hunt down files or change locks after a person leaves. If you didn't have "do not copy" stamped on the keys, then you may want to change the locks if the firing goes poorly and you fear the former employee has made copies of the keys and may take revenge. If there are any company passwords on the computer, or for business email accounts, the business website, a Facebook account, or to do with banking, then you need to change those before you fire the employee.

Firing an employee can be hard, but may be necessary if the person is losing your studio money; is practicing unsafe procedures or not following sanitary codes; or if the person is treating your other employees, yourself, or your clients poorly. Having a bad employee can hurt your business, so if you need to fire someone, do so and stand your ground. Some employees may threaten you or guilt you into trying to take them back, but no bad employee is worth keeping if he or she is causing you grief.

12
Studio Policies

You will need to set up your studio policies and then stick to them in order to remain consistent and keep both your clients and artists happy. Policies you will need to consider implementing include age restrictions for your clients, employee policies, and many others.

You should write a handbook or have a binder of policies available for your staff to consult if they have questions. Having studio rules in writing means that no one can argue that they didn't know about the policies. Every employee should be instructed to read the handbook before their first day of work.

1. Age Restrictions for Tattooing and Piercing

When a person reaches the age of 18, he or she is legally considered an adult in the United States. As of 2010, all states have a federal requirement that the individual receiving a tattoo be an adult at least 18 years of age or older. However, some states do allow for minors to be tattooed with written parental consent.

In Canada, the laws are essentially the same throughout all the provinces and territories. The legal age to consent to receiving a tattoo is 18. Minors must have written parental consent. If a minor is tattooed without a parent or legal guardian's consent, a criminal charge of assault with a deadly weapon can be laid, which can result in jail time for the tattoo artist. It is not legal to accept a brother, sister, aunt, or friend who is older than 18 to sign for the minor, it must be the parent or legal guardian; a legal guardian would have to produce court documents showing proof of this.

Some tattoo artists and studios will allow a parent or guardian to give written consent to have a tattoo performed at a certain age. In all jurisdictions, even those having no law dictating a minimum age, tattoo artists may choose to set age restrictions as a precaution against lawsuits. Seldom will you ever see a tattoo studio offering tattoos to all ages; at least no professional studio, that is. The tattoo artist may also choose to place additional restrictions based on his or her own professional ethics, such as refusing any clients younger than a specific age even with parental consent, or limiting the type and/or body location he or she is willing to tattoo a minor (such as refusing any work around intimate parts of the body).

Piercings are not as regulated as tattooing, and some states and provinces don't even have any laws regulating piercing. To find out if there are any laws in regards to piercing in your area contact your local health authority. Most studios will set the age between 16 and 18 to avoid runs-ins with angry parents and or/civil lawsuits. Canada has no law regulating what age an individual can be pierced but local health authorities almost all ask for a minimum age of 16 if there's no parental consent.

Most studios, if they perform genital piercings and dermal anchors, will set an age of 18 if there's no parental consent; age restrictions are highly recommended to avoid any

problems. In most areas it is illegal to perform genital piercings on a minor.

2. Employee Policies

Employee polices can be tricky, as almost all tattooists and piercers are independent or subcontractors. This is why a contract signed at the start of employment can help avoid many problems and questions that may arise later. Since these positions are subcontracted, you will not be able to expect the typical employer/employee relationship. For example, what happens when the tattoo artist had a solid day booked with tattoo appointments and one of the appointments does not show up for a two-hour session? Unless it is specified in a contract, the artist can leave the studio and come back in two hours for his or her next appointment. Also, there are days when there are no appointments booked. What if the artist decides to take a day off, rather than coming in, missing potential walkins? Different scenarios should be addressed in your employee contracts, and reminders should be noted in your employee handbook.

There are some positives to having subcontracted artists, such as the financial benefits if you have a slow day where the studio makes little to no money; then there is no hourly rate to be paid, and you avoid the costly expense of paying employee taxes, holiday pay, and statutory holiday pay.

It is recommended that strict policies on workstations or rooms be enforced as to artists and piercers leaving them clean and sterile after every use.

Another important policy is the price you will set for the tattoo artists' and the piercers' friends and family to get work done at your studio. Setting too high a price for friends and family will cause them to tattoo or pierce behind your back, whether it be in your studio or at someone's house. Setting too low a price will cause you to lose money on supplies and energy.

Also the time when the friends and family get procedures done is important because, on the one hand, if it is not on the artist's day off, you miss out on paying clients and you lose time on the room. On the other hand, if it is done on a day off, the piercer or tattoo artist could become burnt out for the upcoming work week.

On the piercing side you will want to decide whether or not you will sell your employees, friends, and family jewelry at cost or for a slight mark-up or full price. Keep in mind, as discussed in Chapters 9 and 10, regardless of the arrangements between you and your staff, your clients will always view the studio as a whole, good or bad.

It is a good idea to have a policy in place if tattoo artists and piercers you have hired are late for their appointments or do not show up at all. You can, of course, let them go or put them on probation, but a better method is to offer a discount to the client that the artist or piercer was late for and then take the discount off the artist's percentage of pay. If the artist does not show up at all, you can offer the client the full discount of the artist's or piercer's percentage and try to rebook the client. A phone call from the absentee piercer or artist to the client also demonstrates to the client that your studio values his or her business. Implementing policies that make the tattoo artist or piercer accountable tend to work better than scare tactics of nonemployment.

3. Dealing with the Theft of Artwork

In today's tattoo industry the demand is high for custom artwork. Custom art is designed for each client based on his or her requests and requirements for a tattoo. Most clients will want to see a drawing before they book an appointment for the tattoo. Some will request that you email the drawing or let them take it home to look at, which can lead to theft of the artwork. Some clients will take the drawing to other studios and find the least expensive price to get the tattoo done, so you lose the potential booking and the artist gets nothing for the time it took to create the piece, unless you charge in advance for all custom drawings.

Charging in advance for customer drawings has both positive and negative aspects. Some clients don't want to pay to see what they may decide not to have placed on their bodies, and others feel they can take up large amounts of the artist's time with phone calls and visits because they've "prepaid" for it. Both situations can lead to a loss of clientele. On the positive side some clients take the process more seriously because there has been an exchange of money, and those who are willing to invest in the creation stage of a tattoo are usually more willing to invest in the finished product.

When dealing with a client from out of town, or a client who has physical difficulties that makes it difficult for him or her to visit your studio many times to look at various drawings and changes, it is often advantageous not to email the drawings but instead to tell the client you will keep the drawings on file until he or she can get back in to see them, whenever that may be.

4. Consultations

Consultations are offered by the tattoo studio to clients before tattoo appointments. The clients bring in any reference they might have and discuss their ideas with the tattoo artist.

The tattooist gives a price and time estimate and what he or she can and cannot do in regards to the tattoo desired.

Consultations take about 20 to 30 minutes and can involve the tattoo artist drawing on the client with sharpie markers to show examples of placement and shape. If a drawing is needed usually this can take from one to two weeks depending on how busy the tattoo artist is at the time, then the client comes back to look at the drawing and offer his or her opinions then changes can be made, if any. At this point a tattoo appointment is usually made by the client.

Some studios charge for the consult and some do not. You must look at your business plan and decide if it would be considered a double charge or would be accepted by your clients. It is recommended from experience that any reference or images brought in by clients be photocopied and returned to the clients immediately to avoid any lost artwork, especially if it is a photograph, which may be irreplaceable.

5. Touch-ups and Follow-ups

Touch-ups and follow-ups are required for some tattoos after the tattoos are healed. They can be for a multitude of reasons and sometimes, when something goes wrong, it's very hard to determine what exactly went wrong. The tattoo could be missing a line or maybe some of the color did not hold well or some spots could be missing color altogether. Touch-ups are required more often due to the client's fault and not the artist's fault.

However, if a client soaks in water before his or her tattoo is healed, this will fade the color of the tattoo causing it to look old and could also cause an infection if it was in an ocean, lake, or hot tub. If the client sun tans during the healing process, the tattoo color

will fade. When the tattoo is healing it will get some scabs on it. Since the scabs are extremely itchy a client may pick at and remove them, which can lift out some of the ink that is attached to the scab and cause the spot to lose color.

Some clients will react with a certain color of ink, and the ink will reject due to an allergic reaction. Improper cleaning and aftercare products can also cause the tattoo ink to fade or reject during the healing process. It is best to use or recommend products that have the least amount of chemical and synthetic additives. Products that have perfumes, intensive moisturizers, and acne or oil removers are not recommended as they can cause tattoo ink to reject in the healing stage.

Determining why ink faded or rejected in an improperly healed tattoo can be very difficult and the client will usually not be forthcoming in admitting any fault.

Sometimes touch-ups are required because of the technique used by the tattoo artist, such as missing a line or spot to color in. The artist could have worked the skin too hard, gone too deep, or tried to blend too many colors in one sitting. All of these factors can cause ink rejection or fading.

Most tattoo artists will ask the client to come back when the tattoo is healed so they can see what it looks like and to get a picture for their portfolios. This way you can also see how the tattoo healed and gauge your tattooist's work.

Usually there is a nominal fee charged for touch-ups. Consult your artist to determine a fair price for his or her time after a piece has been completed, and decide at the beginning whether all touch-ups will be treated the same regardless of circumstance.

Some studios allow for free touch-ups to be performed for up to a year after the initial tattoo was done. It all depends on the studio, how busy it is, and if they want to provide this service for free or not. Many customers like this added bonus and it will keep them coming back.

6. Fixing Another Tattoo Artist's Work

When a client is unhappy with a tattoo, he or she may never return to the artist or studio, so you will have clients coming in to your studio with tattoos that they want fixed by you or one of your artists. Not all tattoo artists will touch another's work so be aware of what your tattoo artists will and will not do. This is due in great part to when a tattoo needs to be fixed; it will not always turn out as good as it could have on a clear canvas. Therefore, the tattoo artist and your studio may not want your names attached to a non-original piece.

Sometimes the tattoo is simply unfixable. In this case a cover-up may be the client's best option. There is an increasing market for cover-ups as the industry evolves towards tattoos being an expression of higher art forms, and away from traditional pick and stick images.

7. Portfolios

Portfolios are what the public will look through when at your studio. This is where most clients will make the final decision on whether or not they will get a tattoo at your studio. It will also help determine which artist, if you have more than one, they will choose for their tattoo or piercing. Portfolios determine for the client the level of skill your artists offer, so it is recommended that only the best of their artwork be on display.

When it comes to piercing it has been my experience that most clients look at the portfolios when they cannot decide on which piercing to pick or the placement and style of the jewelry.

A portfolio should have large pictures and preferably one per page. The portfolio should be in good repair with no torn edges or pages. In the portfolios you will want the artist and piercers to display a wide variety of tattoos and piercings. This shows the public that your artists have a good knowledge base and a wide range of abilities. Limiting a portfolio to the artist's favorite style or piercing will look to the public as if the person is limited in his or her skills. The smaller the city or town, the more varied you and/or your tattoo artists will have to be.

8. Restrictions

Amongst professional piercers there is a well-known adage that states, "If you can pinch it, you can pierce it." For the most part this is true. There are a few piercings that are not recommended due to the damage that may be inflicted on the client who receives them, the most dangerous of these being —

- cheeks or dimples, as this can cause a punctured parotid duct or gland which can cause lasting and permanent disability;
- eyelid piercings, for obvious reasons;
- horizontal tongue, which can cause excessive bleeding and nerve damage;
- an "outie" navel piercing, which can cause herniation and peritonitis; and
- subclavicle, which means beneath the collar bone; this can cause uncontrollable bleeding and nerve damage.

In regards to tattoos, anywhere on the body including the eyelids can be tattooed, but not all places are recommended or will be considered a good canvas choice by every tattoo artist. Note that in some jurisdictions you cannot tattoo the face, for such as cosmetic tattooing of the eyebrows, eyelids, or lips. See Chapter 6 for more on rules and regulations.

Body parts that are not recommended to be tattooed include the bottom of the feet because it is extremely painful and the tattoo will rarely hold, meaning it will have to redone throughout the person's life to keep the tattoo visible. The hands, ears, and lips are also fragile tissue areas, ones that will need touch-ups or reworking constantly to keep tattoos looking vibrant and solid. It is wise to be aware of this with touch-ups in these areas; some studios have an additional charge on touch-ups on the hands and feet because they will constantly need touch-ups.

In regards to private areas of the body, it is up to the studio and the tattoo artists' discretion whether they will or will not tattoo these areas. The same goes for piercings as not all studios will pierce genitals; again it just depends on the piercers' and the studio's discretion.

9. Dealing with Last-Minute Cancellations

Most tattoo studios will require a deposit for tattoo appointments. The price of this depends on the studio and the length of time the tattoo is booked for. The deposit goes toward the tattoo and helps guarantee that the client will show up. If the client does not show up or phone, the deposit is kept and split between the owner and the tattoo artist, usually on the same percentage of pay that the tattoo artist would get for a tattoo. The gray area is when the client phones the same day to cancel his or her appointment; at this point do you return the deposit, keep the deposit, or move the deposit to a new appointment day? If the time slot is canceled it cannot be filled because of such short notice, so you and the tattoo artist lose out on that time; in this case it would seem fair to keep the deposit. However, the client can find that action unfair because he or she has to pay another deposit. It is best to play each situation separately or have a set policy that states a certain time frame such as if the client does not phone or cancel within 24 hours then the deposit is kept.

It is very rare for a studio to take deposits for piercings as they are usually booked in 15- to 30-minute intervals and appointment slots can be filled easier than tattoo ones, which usually require a consult prior to the actual tattoo, and more hours being booked depending on the size of the art. It is a good idea to keep a cancellation list of clients who want in that day for a tattoo or piercing if there is a cancellation, as this can help with last-minute cancellations.

10. Creating Aftercare Instructions for Clients

Aftercare instructions are a must to give to clients when they leave the studio. It entails all the information on how to clean a tattoo or piercing, what products to clean the artwork with, information on things to avoid and what not to do, tips to increase healing times, troubleshooting, and contact information. These sheets must be comprehensive and cover all relevant topics to the tattoo or piercing received.

When a client leaves your studio there are numerous aftercare instructions that must be followed if the tattoo or piercing is to heal properly, so you will want the tattoo artist and the piercer to go over aftercare with the client as well as send the person home with printed instructions. This is important for the health of the client as well as the image of your studio, because if a client does not follow the aftercare and the tattoo or piercing does not heal properly and looks bad, then your studio is associated with that. Also if the client gets an infection, his or her health can be at risk. For example, if a client goes into a hot tub with a fresh piercing or tattoo, he or she risks a staph infection (Staphylococcus aureus) which can be very serious.

Research your aftercare methods and rely on the expertise of your tattoo artist and piercer as well as keeping up to date in new techniques and products released.

Samples 9 and 10 include aftercare instructions for tattoos and piercings. The CD also includes a copy of these instructions for you to tweak to suit your studio.

11. How to Schedule Appointments

Scheduling can be very difficult especially with tattoo appointments. The best way to get a more accurate time for tattoo appointments is to have the client book a consult with the tattoo artist; the tattoo artist can better gauge how long the tattoo will take better than you or your receptionist. Even with consults the time of tattoos can exceed or be less than the time allotted due to a number of factors such as the client needing more breaks than anticipated, the skin of the client is not taking the ink well, the client changing his or her mind on the size or design of the tattoo last minute, and interference by friends or family who may accompany the client. It is wise to always book more time

for the tattoo than expected because of these reasons as well include time for tear down, set-up, and sterilization of the room or workspace, before and after the procedure.

Piercings are usually booked in 15- to 30-minute time blocks depending on the piercing and if it is more than one piercing or a dermal anchor. Time can vary with piercings as well, mostly due to nervousness of the clients and having to relax them before the procedure can begin.

Keep in mind that you do not want to overwork or underwork your tattoo artists or piercers. Getting to know their likes and dislikes in regards to client flow and their rate of speed when performing procedures can help immensely when scheduling appointments.

12. Set up a Cleaning Schedule

Every artist and piercer must clean up their workstation after every appointment. However, you will need to make sure your front waiting area is clean as well. You may want to set up a cleaning schedule for your receptionist or you to do.

Cleaning tasks may include the following:

- Sweeping and mopping floors.
- Organizing portfolios and display cases.
- Cleaning front window glass and glass cases.
- Cleaning and sanitizing the bathroom.
- Using antibacterial spray to wipe door handles and any other surfaces clients may touch.

(Note that some clients may touch their tattoo or piercing and then touch other surfaces,

Sample 9
Tattoo Aftercare Instructions

(Insert your business name and contact information at the top of the instructions.)

Leave Dry-Lock bandage on for a minimum of 4 hours to a maximum of 10 hours. This allows your skin to build up its protective layer against bacteria and germs. When you remove the bandage there will be ink on it — this is normal!

Wash hands with an antibacterial soap before removing bandage. Never re-bandage tattoo.

Wash tattoo with a neutral soap such as Neutrogena. Gently use your hands to rub soap over tattoo. *Never* use a washcloth. Always wash hands before cleaning tattoo.

Pat dry tattoo with a towel. *Never* rub your tattoo dry. This will help avoid pulling any of the ink out of the skin that may be attached to a scab.

Clean your tattoo 3 to 5 times a day until healed.

When the tattoo begins to scab and dry out, apply lotion. You want to keep the tattoo moist but not wet. When choosing a lotion you must choose one with no fragrances, and no acne or oil removers. We recommend that you use Lubriderm or Moisturel, which are both a basic dry skin lotion with no additives that may react with your tattoo. We have found that some intensive dry skin lotions contain additives that react with tattoo ink causing the ink to reject.

Average healing time is anywhere from 7 to 14 days.

Never pick your scabs no matter how itchy they may become. Lightly slap the tattoo to get rid of the itch.

Touch-ups are free for one year except for feet and hand tattoos which have a $25 touch-up fee.

Additional Information

You may shower 4 hours after receiving the tattoo. However, do not shower in really hot water and not for an extended period of time, meaning no longer than 15 minutes. No baths or swimming (e.g., lakes, hot tubs, or swimming pools) because this will cause your tattoo color to fade. As well lake water may contain bacteria that may cause an infection to the tattooed area. You may bathe and swim as soon as your tattoo is completely healed, meaning no scabs.

You must keep your tattoo out of the sun and away from tanning beds until you are healed. The sun and tanning beds will fade the color in your tattoo faster than anything else. When you are healed we strongly recommend applying sunscreen to your tattoo any time it is exposed to the sun.

You must take time off from training, working out, or any intense physical activity until you are healed. Profuse sweating has the same effect on your tattoo as soaking in water.

You do not need to apply Polysporin, Bactine, or any other chemical products to your tattoo. Soap and water along with oxygen will heal your tattoo faster than anything that contains chemicals and synthetics. Chemical products will cause a longer healing time and may react with your tattoo ink.

SELF-COUNSEL PRESS — START & RUN A TATTOO & BODY PIERCING STUDIO/11

Sample 10
Piercing Aftercare Instructions

(Insert your business name and contact information at the top of the instructions.)

How Your Piercing Heals Is up to You!

Congratulations! You've just received a body piercing by a trained professional who cleaned and disinfected the pierced area and used sterilized needles, piercing instruments, and jewelry. Now it is up to you to take appropriate care of your piercing.

Warning: Chemicals will not make you heal faster! In fact, quite the opposite. Chemicals of any kind will upset the balance within your newly forming tissue cells and create a condition in which your piercing will heal slower, if ever. Therefore, do *not* use *any* product marked "For External Use Only" including, but not limited to the following:

- Provon
- Rubbing alcohol
- Hydrogen peroxide
- Bactine
- All ear-care solutions (e.g., benzalkonium or benzethonium chloride)
- Antibacterial products (e.g., Liquid Dial, Softsoap, Neosporin)
- Any petroleum-based ointment
- Betadine (i.e., povidone-iodine)
- Hibiclens

Products You Can Use:

- Non-iodized sea salt. You can find this at a health-food store and it's usually better quality than what grocery stores sell. (Do *not* use table salt or Epsom salt.)
- Saline solution. Saline is the key to quick healing. The easiest and most accurate way to acquire saline is in the form of saline solution for contact lenses. Preferably, the sterile type in a pressurized can. (Do *not* use contact-cleaning solutions or soaking/wetting solutions.)
- Pick up some Q-tips, especially when you have a piercing (e.g., nostril) where getting at the inside may be difficult.

How to Clean Your Piercing:

Important: Always wash your hands before touching your body piercing.

Mix one teaspoon of non-iodized sea salt with 8 ounces/1 cup of warm water. Arrange this solution so that you soak the piercing (e.g., put a shot glass over your navel or nipple and then lie back letting the piercing soak). Leave the warm salt-water solution there until it is cold, then rinse the piercing with saline solution. After soaking, use cotton balls, Q-tips, or gauze, to clean the area of the piercing. Gently clean any lymph (crusties) away from the piercing. Do this several times a day until your piercing is completely healed.

Do *not* move the jewelry back and forth through the piercing. This does more harm than good. It is always okay to gently rinse the outside of a piercing with saline and a clean Q-tip. Do this when activity may cause the ring to turn (e.g., exercise) or when it feels "sticky" or uncomfortable.

SELF-COUNSEL PRESS — START & RUN A TATTOO & BODY PIERCING STUDIO/11

Some people have good luck cleaning the outside of their piercing and ring in the shower with a diluted high-quality glycerin or Castile-based soap. Make sure you rinse afterwards with saline.

Some Tips We Have Learned over the Years:

Note for all piercings: Avoid playing with new piercings as a physical irritation is the worst. Leave the piercings alone so they can heal. When clothing is to be in contact, or over the piercing, try to wear clean, loose, and breathable (e.g., cotton) clothes.

Navels: Physical irritation (usually caused by pants rubbing against the jewelry) is the most common navel piercing problem. You must wear your pants and skirt lines below your navel or the piercing may never heal.

Nipples: Many women report that wearing a bra after a nipple piercing helps with soreness, especially for the first few days. Larger breasted women may be more likely to find this true. Wearing a sport-type bra to bed may also help.

Swimming: Chlorine causes new piercings to dry and become irritated and should be avoided if possible. If you cannot avoid swimming, then your best bet is to clean the piercing and rinse with saline after you swim. Avoid hot tubs until the piercings are completely healed. Lakes and oceans are a topic of debate, but a couple of things are certain: Sewage is frequently dumped into these water systems and swimming in sewage is a bad idea! Tropical waters can carry staph infections. However, some people report that their piercing healed instantly after swimming in the ocean. Learn to identify the condition of your piercing and keep it out of irritating situations.

Keloids and scar tissue: 95 percent of the time people mistake irritation for scarring. If you suspect you are developing scar tissue, your piercer or a plastic surgeon is probably the best person to ask for advice.

Miscellaneous Tips:

We don't know how long it will take for your piercing to heal. Some people heal quickly, while others take more time — you will be the best judge of that. Expect new piercings to be sore and red for about a month. If there isn't a marked improvement after that time, contact your piercer to help you determine a route to speed healing. Continue to clean your piercing once a day for as long as you have it.

"Expert" advice: Don't listen to your friend, your mom, or your psychic advisor. We have been doing this far longer than they have! If you have questions, ask your piercer.

Special Care for Oral Piercings:

Lips, cheeks, and tongues require special care. Care for the external part of lip and cheek piercings in the fashion recommended in this instruction sheet.

What you'll need:

- Listerine or non-iodized sea salt to rinse your mouth.
- Ice for tongue and lip piercings — this will reduce swelling.

What to do: Rinse your mouth with Listerine (diluted 50/50 with water) or non-iodized sea salt (¼ teaspoon per cup of water) after you eat, drink, smoke, or put anything in your mouth for the first 2 to 4 weeks. For tongue piercings, gently suck on ice to reduce the swelling.

Tongue: If your tongue is sore and swollen, Ibuprofen may help. Eat slowly and think about chewing. Stay with nonirritating foods (e.g., avoid spicy foods and hot drinks)

SELF-COUNSEL PRESS — START & RUN A TATTOO & BODY PIERCING STUDIO/11

No kissing or sexual contact until completely healed. Gently brush your tongue when you brush your teeth. This will help remove mucus and dead skin.

Lips: Always rinse the piercing with saline solution to keep it balanced and to help it heal faster. Do not play with it!

With labret piercings, you *must* follow up with your piercer in 2 to 4 weeks to have your jewelry checked and/or adjusted. Not doing so could result in gum irritation, or worse, gum recession.

Infected Piercings:

More often than not, people who think they have an infection actually have an irritation and adjusting the method of care will fix the problem. You can recognize a true infection by its relatively sudden inflammation and accompanying discharge of green pus and/or blood. If you suspect that you have an infection, contact your body piercer at once. Do *not* wait for it to get worse and do *not* attempt home remedies.

SELF-COUNSEL PRESS — START & RUN A TATTOO & BODY PIERCING STUDIO/11

which can spread blood and bodily fluids around the studio.)

Part of the tasks may include making sure records and bookkeeping information are up-to-date and organized, as well as checking dates often on sterilized equipment and supplies to make sure nothing has expired.

Clients will notice if they walk into a dirty studio, so make sure yours is always pristine and welcoming.

13. Cleaning and Decontamination of Workstations and Tools

Cleaning and decontamination of work areas and tools should follow Occupation Safety and Health Administration (OSHA) Guidelines and the products to clean with must comply with the Environmental Protection Agency's (EPA's) registered list of disinfectants. Check with your local health authority to obtain a list of approved cleaning products. The entire work area must be cleaned and sterilized before and after each client.

The workstation setup should be done before the client enters the area with everything laid out on the workstation, with all needles and all medical products unopened in their packages. When the client enters the room the tattoo artist or piercer will open the needle and all related equipment in front of the client to offer reassurance that the products are brand new and never have been used before.

13
Dealing with Clients

You should always provide quality customer service to your clients, but what do you do if your client arrives intoxicated? What if your client is violent or verbally abusive? This chapter will help you deal with your clients — the good and the bad.

1. Providing Quality Customer Service

Without clients, you do not have a business. You will want to focus heavily on quality customer service as your clients are providing the income that allows you to pay the bills and keep the studio operating. The old adage "the client is always right" holds significance in the tattoo and piercing industry as well. Although the clients may not always be right, you have to attempt to keep them happy.

Clients will be your best source of advertising whether it be in favor of your studio or against it, so be sure to treat them fairly and professionally to avoid negative word of mouth. The general rule of percentages is that a pleased client will tell one person and a displeased client will tell five or more people. People that have a negative experience are always more vocal about it.

It is important to keep in mind that even though you may have been in this industry for a while or are very well trained and knowledgeable about tattoo and piercing procedures, the majority of clients do not understand all the steps involved in the tattoo and piercing process. Their questions or comments, which to you may seem inane or ridiculous, to them are quiet serious. Sometimes it's just a matter of a client expressing nervousness before a procedure. As the professional it is your job to lessen your client's anxieties, so keep that in mind when answering questions. Always try to remember how it was when you first entered into the industry; as most of us likely did so as clients ourselves. Attempt to make each individual's visit to your studio the experience you had, or maybe the experience you wish you had.

Everyone likes to feel special, so remembering a client's first name or which procedure he or she underwent last time, or something he or she may have said, goes a long way to making a client feel that he or she is more than just a dollar sign to you.

Since a tattoo or piercing requires the use of needles most people become extremely nervous. This is magnified if it is their first procedure so calming clients and answering their questions and concerns should be a routine part of client service. Just being sincere and acknowledging their nervousness and going over the aftercare of the tattoo or piercing in depth will show the clients you care about their well being. Don't belittle customers who are nervous.

Make sure the client knows he or she can call the studio anytime for any advice or help he or she may require after he or she leaves your studio, showing again that you are not just interested in getting the person's money, but that you care about how the tattoo and/ or piercing is healing and the person's health.

A good practice for first-time clients is to give them a tour of your studio, pointing out the health-board certification, and other relevant documentation. This will give the clients

something else to focus on by receiving an education, as well as give you the opportunity to demonstrate your studio's professionalism.

2. Clients Who Are Unhappy with the Work

Unhappy clients can tarnish a studio's reputation, thus losing you potential revenue, so handling each situation with due care and diligence is of the utmost importance. For example, if a client is unhappy with a piercing and thinks that it is crooked or does not look right, the best practice is to offer to redo the piercing at no charge to the person. This demonstrates that you care about the quality of work that comes out of your studio. In reality it is far more cost effective to redo a piercing than risk the backlash of an angry client who could deter future clients from entering your studio. If you make a client happy, at your expense, the person will likely return for more procedures in the future and he or she will usually bring friends or family.

Refunding a customer's money is a last resort option and should only be done when all other measures have failed. At its basic level a studio's primary function is to offer a service. If, as the owner, you can absolutely verify that the procedure was done correctly and to the best ability of your staff, there is never a reason to refund for services rendered. In the extreme case of a client threatening legal action it would be your choice to obtain legal counsel and/or refund the money.

With piercings, many times the client will mistake irritation or certain stages of the healing process with infection and will call or come into your studio irate that his or her piercing is "infected." It is paramount to remember that all such claims must be addressed to make certain that no infection is occurring, and to stand behind any policies of client aftercare. Ninety-nine percent of the time it is simply irritation, but a true infection can be serious so be sure to have you or your piercer take a look at the piercing to make certain that there is no infection present. Do not make clients feel dumb for having asked, but be firm in your assessment of the piercing's health.

For tattoos, if the client is unhappy, it can be a more difficult situation to fix depending on the aspect of the tattoo with which the person is unhappy. If the client does not like a color it can be addressed fairly easy by waiting until the tattoo is healed, then offering the client a free sitting where the tattoo artist will recolor the tattoo with a new color. It is up to the studio and artist whether or not to charge for this, but I would recommend from experience that no charge be issued to the client. If the client is unhappy with the entire tattoo, determine the reason behind this. If the tattoo was done well, no mistakes were made, and the tattoo looks very close to the picture that was agreed upon, then maybe some comprise can be reached where the client will pay to have the tattoo covered up or redone but at a reduced rate.

If a mistake was made by the artist, offer to have the artist fix the tattoo at no charge and offer a sincere apology to the client, explaining that even tattoo artists are human and mistakes can and sometimes do get made.

For tattoos that are text you should have the client sign off on the spelling of it before it is inked. Also for foreign languages and symbols, you should make the client very aware that artists are not translators and cannot guarantee the meaning or spelling of the word. It is not a bad practice to include this on the waiver form that the clients sign so as to avoid any lawsuits or upset clients.

There are many images that do not translate well as tattoos so the artist and or studio must explain this to the client in a professional and non-insulting manner.

Many tattoos are memorial pieces, so extra attention and care must be given to clients who are getting these tattoos as they will tend to be emotional during the tattooing as it brings back memories of their loved ones.

As well, many tattoos seem to be requested when the client is experiencing a milestone in his or her life, or a trauma, and the client can be very excited, depressed, sad, anxious, or angry so be prepared to deal with a wide range of emotions and have respect for what the client is going through.

Clients who request many breaks or will not stop moving during the tattoo have to be dealt with firmly, but not rudely. Make clients aware that if they keep requesting breaks the breaks will be charged as tattoo time. If the client will not stop moving, explain that the tattoo will not turn out well and the tattoo artist and studio cannot be held accountable for this.

3. What to Do If a Client Arrives Intoxicated and Violent or Abusive

Many states and provinces have strict laws that prohibit tattooing or piercing of any individual who is intoxicated on drugs or alcohol. Failure to comply can result in monetary fines or the studio being shut down. These laws are your first line of defense against an intoxicated client as to why the person cannot get tattooed or pierced.

There are also medical reasons as to why a person cannot be tattooed or pierced when intoxicated, such as the fact that the blood is thinner so the person will bleed more causing the tattoo to heal improperly. With new piercings a person will bleed more resulting in a longer healing time.

Intoxicated individuals make unpredictable sudden movements which, during a piercing, can be very unsafe to the piercer and client and during a tattoo can cause broken, misplaced, or crooked lines as well as be unsafe for both the artist and the client.

In regards to decision making, intoxicated people sometimes make wrong choices and tattoos are for life, so sobriety when choosing a tattoo and/or piercing is only smart.

If you have violent and verbally abusive clients, you should ban them from your premises as you have the right to do so as a business owner, and then a police report should be filed. You have every right (and so do your tattoo artists and piercers) to stop or refuse service to anyone who is verbally abusive or violent. Allowing abusive clients to continue to use your services will only result in more problems and unhappy staff.

4. Liability Waiver Forms

Liability waiver forms are a necessity for your business in order to protect yourself, your artists, your piercers, and your studio.

Samples 11 and 12 are examples of tattooing and piercing waivers. We have included copies of these forms on the CD for your use. However, note that you will need to adjust the forms to comply with the laws in your jurisdiction as each area has its own laws and regulations on what should be outlined in a waiver. You would also be wise to have a lawyer review your waiver forms to make sure you comply with all local regulations. It's always better to spend a little money on preventative measures, rather than a lot of money on a lawsuit.

Sample 11
Consent to Application of Tattoo Waiver/Release Form

Please place a checkmark beside all ten points. If any point is not understood, please ask any representative or independent contractors of _____
(insert studio name and address) before the tattoo is started.

1. ❏ I am not a hemophiliac (bleeder). I do not have diabetes, epilepsy, hepatitis, HIV, AIDS, or any communicable disease. I am not under the influence of alcohol and/or drugs.

2. ❏ I acknowledge that it is not reasonably possible for the representatives and independent contractors of _____ *(insert name of studio)* to determine whether I might have an allergic reaction to the pigments or process used in my tattoo, and I agree to accept the risk that such a reaction is possible.

3. ❏ I acknowledge that infection is always possible as a result of obtaining a tattoo, particularly in the event that I do not take proper care of my tattoo. **I will follow the aftercare instructions provided to me.** I agree that any touch-up work required because of my own negligence, will be done at my own expense.

4. ❏ I realize that variations in color and design may exist between any tattoo as selected by me and as ultimately applies to my body. I understand that if my skin color is dark, the colors will not appear as bright as they do on lighter colored skin.

5. ❏ I acknowledge that the artists are not translators and cannot guarantee the spelling or meaning of foreign words or symbols. I confirm that the spelling of any words to be used for the tattoo are correct and to my liking.

6. ❏ I acknowledge that a tattoo is a permanent change to my appearance and that no representations have been made to me as to the ability to later change or remove my tattoo. To my knowledge, I do not have any physical, mental, or medical impairment or disability which might affect my well-being as a direct or indirect result of my decision to have any tattoo-related work done at this time.

7. ❏ I acknowledge that I have truthfully represented to the independent contractors and representatives of_____ *(insert studio name)* that I am of the age of eighteen (18) or older and that the following information is true and correct.

8. ❏ I acknowledge that obtaining my tattoo is by my choice alone and I consent to the application of the tattoo and to any action or conduct of the independent contractors and representatives of _____ *(insert studio name)* necessary to perform the tattoo procedure.

9. ❏ I agree to release and forever discharge and hold harmless_____ *(insert studio name)* and all its independent contractors from any and all claims, damages, and legal actions arising from or connected in any way with my tattoo and the procedures and conduct used to apply my tattoo.

10. ❑ I give permission to the artists and studio to use pictures of my tattoo for portfolio displays as well as for advertising purposes on the studio's website and in all other marketing materials.

YOU MUST BE AT LEAST 18 YEARS OLD

Please Print

Name:_____ Phone:_____

City:_____ State/Province:_____ Zip/Postal Code:_____

Date of birth:_____ Age:_____

(Note: You must show valid government identification before you will receive your tattoo.)

Signature:_____

Date:_____

Where did you hear about our studio?_____

For Studio Use Only:

Body design and location of tattoo:_____

Artist:_____

Total Amount Due: $_____

Would you like to be on our enewsletter mailing list? (Note that by giving us your email address you give us permission to contact you. You can opt out at any time by using the opt-out link in the enewsletter.) If so, please provide your email address here: _____

Sample 12
Consent to Body Piercing Procedure Waiver/Release Form

To allow_____ (insert name of piercer) to pierce my_____ (describe area to be pierced) and in consideration of all its doing, I hereby release *him/her* and all agents from all manner of liabilities, claims, actions, and demands, in law or in equity which I or my heirs have or might have now or hereafter by reason of complying with my request to be pierced.

I understand that I will be pierced using appropriate instruments and techniques to ensure proper healing of my piercing(s) and I agree to follow the procedures outlined in the suggested aftercare instructions until healing is complete. I understand that this type of piercing usually takes_____ (insert length of time it usually takes for this type of piercing to heal) or longer to heal.

YOU MUST BE AT LEAST 18 YEARS OLD

Please Print

Name:_____ Phone:_____

City:_____ State/Province:_____ Zip/Postal Code:_____

Date of birth:_____ Age:_____

(Note: You must show valid government identification before you will receive your piercing.)

Signature:_____

Date:_____

Where did you hear about our studio?_____

Would you like to be on our enewsletter mailing list? (Note that by giving us your email address you give us permission to contact you. You can opt out at any time by using the opt-out link in the enewsletter.) If so, please provide your email address here: _____

Must Read and Sign if jewelry was not purchased at_____ (insert name of studio).

New piercings require jewelry that is a high-quality metal such as stainless steel 316L, 316LVM, or Titanium Grade 23. If you have purchased your jewelry elsewhere, we cannot guarantee that your jewelry is of this quality.

Low-quality jewelry contains materials that are toxic to the body. Due to this fact, you agree that _____ (insert name of studio) or any of its subcontracted employees will not be held responsible for any problems that could arise from using jewelry not purchased at_____ (insert name of studio).

Signature:_____ _____

Print name:_____

For Studio Use Only:

Description of jewelry purchased: _____ Cost $_____

_____ $_____

_____ $_____

Piercing fee: $_____

Total Amount Due: $_____

SELF-COUNSEL PRESS — START & RUN A TATTOO & BODY PIERCING STUDIO/11

14 Final Considerations

Once you have your business up and running, this chapter will help you decide what steps to take next.

1. Things to Consider before Expanding Your Business

After you have been in business for a few years, and you feel it is doing well, you may want to consider expanding your studio or moving to a bigger location. There are a number of reasons to expand your studio including:

- The current lease for the building you rent is about to expire and your landlord wants to increase the rate to something that is not in your budget.

- Your studio needs to hire more artists to accommodate the target market's demands.

- You need to move into a better studio that provides more space or you've found a better location.

- You want to open a second location in another area of a big city and expand your brand.

- You want to add new services for clients and will be partnering with hairstylists, estheticians, massage therapists, etc.

There are many reasons to expand a business, but the most important thing to remember is to budget for the expansion. Don't get in over your head with lofty dreams. In essence, it is like starting out as a new business in that you have to make sure you have a sound business plan for the new or improved business. Consider the following questions:

🌹 Will you be able to dedicate more time to the business, which means less time for family?

🌹 Do you have the finances or investors in place for the expansion or will you have to use your savings?

🌹 Will the investment in expanding be worth it?

🌹 Can you afford to close your studio for a week or two (or longer) to do the renovations needed for expansion?

🌹 Have you found good employees that will fit in with current employees?

🌹 Can you afford the extra costs for utilities and property taxes?

🌹 If you are opening a second studio, will you have the staff to fill that location?

If you are thinking of a second studio, you will need to hire someone to manage it; otherwise, you will run yourself ragged trying to cover duties for both studios. This is when things get forgotten and problems will arise causing you more stress and headaches.

Opening a second location means creating a new business plan, marketing plan, and advertising campaign, which all cost time and money. You may want to talk to a business consultant or someone who specializes in business expansion before you go ahead with your plans. Having a professional's opinion can mean the difference between success and failure.

1.1 Moving to a new location

If you are moving locations, then you will have to have a solid advertising campaign to make sure your clients and potential clients know where to find you. You need to start advertising your move many weeks, if not months in advance to prepare your clients for the change.

You will more than likely lose some customers from your move. One of the reasons could be because a new studio (different owner) takes over your old premises, which means some customers may go there looking for your studio and decide they like the new studio.

One measure that can be taken is to offer the new tenant of your old location money to let your clients know where your new location is. If it is not rented or bought, then leave a sign in the window or door that lets the clients know where to find your studio.

It's important to contact your current customers either by phoning them or through social media outlets such as Facebook, MySpace, and Twitter to let them know where your new location will be. If you include on your waiver forms a spot for clients' email addresses, then email can be a great way to contact all your old and existing clients about the move. You may also want to offer discounts or free merchandise to those who book appointments within the first few weeks of opening at your new location. Also, a grand reopening with live music or some other event can be a great way to reach clients and have a fun day.

2. Succession Planning

Succession planning means setting up your business so that someone else can take over if you are not able to continue as the owner and operator. For example, what happens if you have an accident or get sick or even die? What will happen to the business you built?

If you are the sole owner and artist in your studio, it will be slightly more difficult to plan for someone else to take it over. The business has been built around you and you are the brand. However, if you have a shop with many artists, you may want to put plans together for who will run your business if the worst happens.

You may have a family member who will need to be taken care if you die, so having income from the studio, or for your family to be able to sell the business may be important considerations in your succession planning.

If you are in a partnership or the business is incorporated, your succession planning should have been taken care of at the time contracts were drawn. However, if you run a sole proprietorship, can your spouse or a child of legal age take over the business for you? Does the person want to take over the business or would he or she rather sell it?

Maybe you already have a plan in place with certain key employees to take over management if you retire or become too ill to tend to the business. Illness or injury can strike at any time so your key employees will have to be trained in all your duties to take over immediately if something should happen to you.

Being that tattooing can sometimes be a transient profession, you are going to have to make sure you aren't training the wrong person, such as a person who will take all the training and then quit and open his or her own business. You have to go with your instinct on who will be a loyal person that wants to stay on and run the business.

Talk to an attorney who specializes in succession planning to see what would work for your studio. The important thing to remember is to put a plan in place before you are forced to make any decisions, or before something happens where you can no longer make those decisions.

3. Trying New Things — Keeping up with Industry Changes

It is important to keep on top of industry changes and updates in regulations. If you can show that your studio is on top of trends and new industry advances, you will secure your studio as the place to go.

In order to keep up with the times you should always be reading industry magazines and websites. Also, going to tattoo conventions will introduce you to new innovations in the industry. Talking to other studio owners and artists in your network will also provide you with information. Researching regulations and talking with studios in other countries can be beneficial too, as they may have a new product or procedure that is not even offered yet in your country and the knowledge or purchase of it will set you ahead of all other studios.

Most important, always be aware of ever-changing government regulations. Get a contact within your local health authority who can provide you with updates to laws and regulations as they happen. Your clients will appreciate that you care and want to make sure your studio is following all the rules out there that keep them safe.

Research can sometimes lead to more efficient practices, which in the long run can create higher revenues. For example, the development of disposable tattoo and piercing tools has eliminated the need for sterilization and cleaning of these tools and frees up about one hour of time each day that can be used for tattooing or piercing, which in turn leads to more money.

Another example of industry change is the development of dermal anchoring, a new piercing procedure. Studios that were on top of this development did the research and practice ahead of other studios, which financially benefited them since they were the first in their areas to offer the new and now widely demanded dermal anchoring procedure. It basically made those studios the first experts on the procedure and secured their studios as the places to go to by their customers.

Being the first to offer new services sets you apart from other studios, and you can charge more for the services because none or very few studios offer them. Be careful in charging too much though as other studios will in time catch on and hire trained professionals to provide the services; and those studios may end up charging less. You do not want your clients to feel as though they have been overcharged for a service or product.

With the ever-increasing popularity of tattoos and piercings, clients are becoming more educated themselves and having a client know about a new product or procedure before you do can be embarrassing as well as bad for business.

Researching new trends and changes can lead to innovative ideas for your studio that you may have not thought of otherwise. Be sure to take your time and research new products and procedures as sometimes they are not better than the traditional methods, or may only last

a limited amount of time in public demand and the investment in the new product or service might outweigh any sales gained. For example, demand for certain body jewelry products can change extremely quickly, and if you have a high amount of inventory of a certain type of body jewelry that is no longer popular, you will having trouble selling excess stock.

Be careful when dealing with body jewelry sales representatives as they will push new products and say they have sold thousands and that certain items are the "new best thing." This is not always the case. For instance, a new type of navel jewelry was developed that offered the client the option of changing the ends with a pin insertion method, somewhat like an ear stud. This product cost four times more at wholesale than traditional navel pieces and never caught on with the public, resulting in many studios being stuck with navel pieces they could never sell.

Be aware that offering a new piercing or tattooing procedure might require travel to another country, state or province, or city for you to take the training, so be sure to weigh the costs of training and learning against the profit that will be gained from it.

Basically, you should never stop learning and researching new trends, ideas, products, health guidelines, and services. If you do become complacent in learning new things, it will eventually lead to a loss in clients and revenues. Staying on top of industry changes will keep your studio ahead of the pack by offering your clients the best and safest tattoo and piercing procedures available.

Employee Management for Small Business

Lin Grensing-Pophal

ISBN: 978-1-55180-863-5

$20.95 USD/$23.95 CAD

Finding and keeping good employees is crucial to the success of every business, but it's not easy. This book will show small-business owners how to develop a human resources plan tailored to their needs.

From hiring and orientation to developing company policies and negotiating employment contracts, this book covers the essentials of employee management.

Like all the books in the 101 for Small Business series, each topic in the book is explained in simple language and is illustrated with real-world examples, checklists, and forms..

Also included is a CD-ROM with all the employee management forms a small business will need. These ready-to-use forms were specially designed to save managers time. You can print out as many copies as you need, and you can even customize them to suit your business. Forms are included in PDF and MS Word formats **for use on a Windows-based PC.**

Manage Your Online Reputation

Tony Wilson

ISBN: 978-1-77040-056-6

$18.95 USD/$19.95 CAD

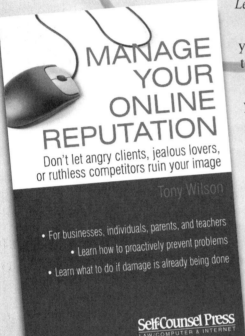

Learn how to protect yourself ... from yourself!

What are people saying about you, your business, or your children online? If you're being slandered on the Internet, what can you do to stop the damage?

A negative reputation can have harmful effects on your business and personal relationships. It is becoming increasingly important for companies and individuals to be able to effectively manage their online reputations. While businesses are springing up to help corporate customers deal with online reputation management issues, most small businesses, parents, and individuals will need to do the work themselves; and very few will have any idea how to do it.

In *Manage Your Online Reputation*, author and lawyer Tony Wilson guides readers through possible issues and the steps to take to prevent or avert issues if negative things are being said about you, your business, or even your children on the Web.

You will learn:

- How to monitor what people are saying about you online

- What to do if someone slanders you, your company, or your child on the Internet

- Best practices for Facebook and other social sites

- How to be proactive and manage your online legacy going forward

Self-Counsel Press

Finance & Grow Your New Business

Angie Mohr

ISBN: 978-1-55180-820-8

$19.95 USD /$23.95 CAD

- Raise capital for your small business
- Measure risk and plan for profitability
- Grow your small business profitably

Entrepreneurs need to know how to measure the effectiveness of their operations, human resources, and marketing in order to pinpoint inefficiencies and maximize profits. This book outlines all the ways to raise capital and then make it work for you!

Many small business owners aren't able to take that next big step in expanding operations. This book shows you how to raise money to finance expansion, how to analyze key factors in your financial information and develop ratios of return on investment that will indicate the direction you should take your business.

Finance & Grow Your New Business explains, in easy-to-understand terms, how to get the money you need for your business, and how to grow your business profitably.

Self-Counsel Press

Commercial Lease Agreements

ISBN: 978-1-55180-774-4

$19.95 USD/$19.95 CAD

Anyone who owns commercial property can now handle all aspects of leasing on their own and save significantly on realtor's fees. Whether starting a new lease, subleasing, or renewing a lease, one can easily create a legally binding agreement using the information and forms in this kit.

- Create subleases, renewals, and extensions
- Includes parking space and garage lease agreements
- Professional, ready-to-use forms on CD-ROM

Establish a fully binding agreement for the property and ensure that all the appropriate details are covered in the lease. Contents:

- Lease agreements
- Renewal agreements
- Extension of lease
- Consent to sublease
- Termination of lease
- Monthly rental record
- And more! Instructions included.

JUN 28 2012

Self-Counsel Press